A Change of Pastors

A Change of Pastors

...And How It Affects Change in the Congregation

Loren B. Mead

THE
ALBAN
INSTITUTE

Herndon, Virginia
www.alban.org

The Alban Institute, 2121 Cooperative Way, Suite 100, Herndon, VA 20171

This book is the newly revised and updated edition of *Critical Moment of Ministry: A Change of Pastors* by Loren B. Mead, originally published by the Alban Institute in 1986.

Scripture quotations, unless otherwise noted, are from the New Revised Standard Version of the Bible, © 1989, Division of Christian Education of the National Council of Churches of Christ in the United States of America, and are used by permission.

Cover design by Adele Robey, Phoenix Graphics.

Library of Congress Cataloging-in-Publication Data

Mead, Loren B.
 A change of pastors: and how it affects change in the congregation / Loren B. Mead.— [Rev. ed.].
    p. cm.
 Includes bibliographical references.
 ISBN 1-56699-309-1
 1. Clergy—Appointment, call, and election. I. Title.

 BV664.M38 2005
 253—dc22

                                    2005004586

        09 08 07 06 05   VG   1 2 3 4 5

Contents

Preface

The ideas in this small book are intended to give you help in your leadership of a congregation. But the ideas have a history that may help you understand how to use them. Let me tell you a story. . . .

The story begins for me in 1969 when I got a call from John Hines, then the Presiding Bishop of the Episcopal Church. I was a parish clergyman in North Carolina at the time.

John needed someone to manage a three-year experimental program. I tried to find out what it was all about. "To make parishes grow and get better," was all I could get out of him at first. As I pursued the ideas with him I never got a lot of clarity about them—but they hooked me, because I just *knew* that what went on in local congregations was important. *Very important.*

A committee Bishop Hines had appointed was called the "National Advisory Committee on Evangelism," and it was focusing on the life of congregations. They had already discovered that loads of people came into Episcopal churches, stayed a short while, then disappeared out the back door. They wanted help in figuring out why that was. Their model—one I agreed with—was to figure out how to close the back door.

We named the experiment "Project Test Pattern" (older readers will remember the test pattern that TV stations ran on the screen before programming started—my eldest son still remembers the excitement of watching our seven-inch TV screen on Saturday mornings before the cartoons came on). I think we had a kind of hope that we would discover insights that could move from the test screen to real life. The project started in 1969 and closed December 31, 1974.

I've often thought that we really were using stone-age tools to try to understand and affect the life of religious congregations. Our key commitment was to start with the thing itself—the life of real congregations of real people as they lived. Not "theories of congregations," but the interactions of people and places, of clergy and laity. We hoped we could discover transferable truths and concepts.

We started with an assumption that is commonplace today but was not much accepted in the world of religious denominations then. The assumption was that *congregations are where the rubber hits the road in religious life.* I got involved because I had been pretty vocal and visible making that point.

Quickly we discovered that the issue we had to deal with in every congregation was the relationship between the clergy and the lay leaders of that congregation.

It was not a simple or clear issue. Not only that, we couldn't find much that had been written or known about such relationships. Indeed, not much was known about what actually went on in congregations. Theories abounded. Prejudices abounded. Rumors flew—about how "Old First Church is a mess!" or how "Pastor Jones just got fired!" Nobody seemed to have anything to offer but "old wives' tales" about what leadership was or how to do it, about "honeymoons" for new clergy, about how to deal with church fights and conflicts, about how a church board was supposed to work (but never did), and about how clergy and laity were always at each others' throats.

In the climate of those times, congregations were sort of "necessary evils," the local *thing* that took care of worship and was where church finance came from. It was the thing clergy had to go to when they left seminary because it was the only place they could get jobs. All congregations were related to something more important—called the "conference" or the "diocese" or the "presbytery," or whatever—that "higher" level of the denomination with all the history and tradition and theology that the clergy had studied and that few laypeople knew or cared much about. It is hard to realize that so recently almost no one was focusing on congregations. If that *was* where the rubber hit the road, nobody was talking about it very much.

After the project had a couple of rather spectacular failures, trying things that did not help us understand or improve the lives of congregations, we chose a method of study that was new for us. We began using carefully trained consultants to work with clergy and lay leadership teams on the issues they wanted to deal with. By then, we had discovered that those leaders would only work on the issues they had come to believe were important for them and their congregation. *They* had to identify what to work on.

What had happened by serendipity was that we discovered a method that produced two things at the same time: First, we gained the ability to look at what actually happened inside a congregation, by studying reports from the consultant, where we could see the interactions and track the results. Second, we could build up records of how different change efforts worked, with the ability to see similarities and differences from case to case.

In the long run, it was this ability to see inside the congregation that was the most help. We began publishing narratives of what we discovered in "case stories."

In the final year and a half of that project, we took the method developed earlier to address the issue that is the heart of this book: changing pastors.

What we already knew by then was that in *every* congregation we ran into, the relationship between the clergyperson and the lay leadership team was the critical relationship in the congregation. That relationship, more than any other one thing, determined whether the life of this congregation was going to turn out lay people and clergy who were growing, who were learning, who were moving into deeper understandings of life and of God. That was the critical relationship.

Not only that—we discovered that when the congregation went through a change of the leading clergyperson, there was an extraordinarily pregnant moment at which change could happen. We learned that that was when change *would* happen, powerfully, no matter what—and that the change could go either toward health or toward dysfunction.

In our studies in that year and a half we looked carefully at fifty-three such changes of pastor—we began to identify the different dynamic stages that occurred during that change. This was the beginning of our learning about that particularly critical change point in the dynamics of congregations.

When Project Test Pattern ended, the research on that crucial moment expanded and deepened in the Alban Institute. Even as we worked with many other congregations through this period, we also began working with pastors and lay leaders in the "start-up" period of the first year of a new pastorate. Similarly, we developed and worked with a new breed of "interim pastors" who went into congregations during the "in-between" period, and we found more about those special dynamics. And we learned about clergy firings.

In short, we turned the searchlight onto that moment that comes to all congregations when one pastorate ends and another takes off. Or doesn't. Everything we discovered reinforced our early hunches. That moment is a true moment of pregnancy in which new life can be stillborn or can burst forth with new vibrancy and strength.

Any congregation going through the complex issues that come when one pastor is leaving and as another comes—any such congregation knows that such a time *is* scary, *is* challenging, and *is* full of potential.

This book is intended to be a guide to what we who have engaged in this study over the years have found, a pointer to some of those opportunities, but it is not a "rule book" with rigid dos and don'ts. Everything we encourage people to do we encourage because we've often found that direction promising. Everything we warn you about we warn you because people have gotten in trouble going that way. Every rule in this book deserves to be broken in some situations—indeed, I've helped people do just that. You will find things we never learned—because your situation is unique.

But still, here is a guidebook to help you through a complicated time. I'd like you to consider that we are your companions, and that we'd love to hear what you learn as you go through this critical moment.

Introduction

Years ago, when I first started working with congregations, I discovered that one of the quickest ways to find out "what was what" was to ask people to tell me the story of their congregation.

It wasn't hard. I just asked the question and all sorts of people started telling me the story as they had experienced it. The stories were not all the same, even if the people were talking about the same congregation—some focused on sad or angry parts of the story; others on deep, loving parts of the story. Everyone had experienced the story from their own special viewpoint, and soon we would have a rich, convoluted, contradictory, but deeply touching and meaningful conversation. Many of those conversations were full of laughter and not a few were full of tears.

Early on, though, I noticed that people tended to "remember" their story the way I remember learning history—as if it occurred in terms of dynasties: "When so and so was the king, the country was characterized by . . ." or "During the Ming dynasty, China was . . . ." There was a difference, however. In congregations, the "dynasties" were named for the pastors, not an ancient king or line of potentates:

"Back when Dr. Foster was the pastor, we always used to focus on Bible study."

1

"When Pastor Allison arrived, all of a sudden we had lots of parish dinners and that's when we started Vacation Bible School for the community."

"When Father Johnson was here was when everybody got involved in social programs—feeding the hungry and things like that."

"Mrs. Benedict was the first pastor really to emphasize the Sunday school—we had kids coming out our ears, and we built the education building."

"Pastor Jenson was our 'high church' pastor—that's when we began using liturgical seasons and colors and things like that."

Perhaps our brains depend on that kind of oversimplification. We seem to need to describe the quality of a period of time in our church's story by naming characteristics we attach to the pastoral leader.

The fascinating thing is that people remember that when there was a change of pastor, all the other things changed, too. Indeed, I rarely heard much talk about change in congregations identified with any other single thing. In people's memories, times of changing pastors remind them of the times when "everything" changed. It may just be a trick of memory, but that's what happens. As people look back at their congregation's story, it was when the pastor left and another came that one kind of story ended and another began.

Something quickly struck me: I realized I'd never heard or read about the kind of change people in congregations told me about, and I began to understand why that was. I was a clergyperson, yet I had never experienced or thought about congregations that were "between clergy." I saw that most books about congregations are written by clergy, but no *clergy* have ever been through a change of pastor. OK, so I exaggerate a tiny bit. But very few clergy have been in the shoes of a lay board member or the member of a pastoral search committee, experiencing first hand how traumatic it is for members of a congregation to go through losing one pastor and adjusting to another.

Clergy naturally focus on their own experience—the trauma of leaving a familiar place of work and life, the upsetting of family life, separations from people they care about, and making new connections. In spite of the challenge and excitement of the new position, clergy bring to it some nostalgia or even grief. Clergy know about the anxiety of looking for a call to new work. They experience the pain of a bad job decision. But most do not know how bad it feels to be a member of a congregation and to hear that your pastor is leaving.

When the Alban Institute first did research about what happens when clergy get fired, they seemed to feel it was too harsh, perhaps even un-Christian. Indeed, when we tried to locate examples, knowing very well that many existed, we ran into a stonewall of denial. "We never do that," we heard, or "Our denomination doesn't allow pastors to be fired." So we started gilding the lily just a bit and called it "involuntary termination." It worked pretty well. People talked then.

But a layperson opened my eyes to another, more important emotional issue. He said, "Most of the involuntary terminations I hear about are where congregations really love their pastor and the pastor suddenly tells them, 'I've been called to another position and I'm planning to leave.' *That's* what I call an involuntary termination!" He was right, but I didn't know it until that moment. Laypeople in churches and clergypeople in churches go through the same history, but it feels different depending on where you stand. One reason for this book is to help clergy enter into what parish members go through before the new pastor comes onto the scene.

Second, I want to help sensitize the lay members of the new congregation to something of what happens to the pastor through this change process.

Our focus throughout this book is that critical moment of change when one pastor leaves and another comes, when there is a change of pastorate.

1

The Pastor Is Leaving

"Why did you leave me in this mess?"

The voice on my phone was angry, but I couldn't tell what it was all about, and I didn't recognize who it was.

"What 'mess' are you talking about, and who in the dickens *is* this?" I replied.

"It's Al Shepherdson in Oklahoma City," the voice continued, "and the mess is about the pastor you helped us call to Trinity Church."

The penny dropped, as the English say. Al was a board member from a Presbyterian church I'd worked with about seven or eight years before when they were searching for a new pastor. The congregation was a midsize one with a lot of potential—located not far from a university, filled with people who had ideas and who weren't afraid to take a risk. I had worked with them for about eight months as they were doing their mission study and search and had not heard much from either him or the church for several years. Usually when I don't hear anything from someone for that long, I've found I can expect that things are going along pretty well.

"Al, what kind of 'mess' are you talking about? Last I heard Sarah Brookstone had turned out to be just what the doctor ordered for the congregation." I was trying to get clues to what was going on and why he sounded so angry.

"Oh, she's been doing a top-notch job. No problem there. Only maybe that's *why* I'm angry. She announced to the congregation Sunday that she has accepted another job—and we feel like we're being left in the lurch."

"Come on, then, Al—it's not as if she stole the Sunday collection. Pastors come and go. You know that! When I worked with you several years ago you all were depressed because Bill Townsend had been elected executive presbyter down in Alabama somewhere."

"That was then. This is now," he replied. "Listen—Sarah fooled me. I never thought we'd go for a woman pastor, but she won us over because she was so darned competent. She even got me into a Bible study group, plus I'm back on session again. Not only that, I've agreed to be chair of the long-range planning committee."

"Is *that* the problem?" I asked.

"I guess it is, probably. I'd been *counting* on her. She hooked me back into leadership, and she's made it exciting to rethink our work in this community. She's got us looking to the future, and I'm in the hot seat. How can we do long-range planning when the key leader is bailing out?"

In a half hour Al cooled down a bit and I got a bit more from him. His wife and two teenagers had moved much closer to the church during Sarah's tenure, and it had become a real fixture in their family life. He didn't say it, but I suspect he and his wife are among the major contributors to the parish now as opposed to his rather perfunctory donations in the years when I had first met him.

The fact that their pastor was leaving left him with feelings of betrayal as well as a sense of being left holding the bag. Al was experiencing some genuine anger mixed with regret at losing an important friend.

I know enough about congregations to know that not everybody in Trinity Church was as upset and angry as my friend.

Indeed, I'd be willing to bet there were at least a few who were breathing a sigh of relief at the news. Some of them had never come to terms with having a woman as pastor, and still others resented her straightforward, businesslike manner. "She always wants to get things finished and she doesn't enjoy schmoozing after the meetings are over. I'm not sure she *likes* us," one person had told me. Another commented, "She isn't good with the teenagers."

None of this was a surprise to me. I've been through a lot of pastoral change situations with a lot of congregations and all these responses seem to arise when a pastor decides to go. I'm working from a broader picture from *many* pastoral changes, but Al and his friends at Trinity Church couldn't see past the disruption they were experiencing because of this unexpected resignation. To tell the truth, I'd known it *even on that Thursday night when Sarah had been installed as pastor nearly seven years before*. One day she would leave.

It *does* feel like a disruption when a pastor leaves. Leaders like Al are caught short—all of a sudden the path that had been secure is up for grabs. What are they supposed to do? Who is supposed to do it? Who kept the blueprint?

At Trinity Church, I knew it was likely that some people would get angry enough to take it out on strangers—the same way Al was taking it out on me—or they might blow up in a phone call to the presbytery executive. Some would likely get depressed and stop coming to church for a while. Others would pretend that somehow "somebody" would fix it and a new minister would appear. And still others would just disappear, choosing to go to another church where things are stable, at least until the congregation gets its new pastor. Some of the most faithful members might panic, absolutely convinced that everything will go to pot if they don't get a Jesus Christ look-alike into the pulpit within a month. I also knew—and Al didn't—that many people would probably raise their pledges and buckle down to help the church they loved because they knew they'd be needed more now.

I had known that Sarah would leave in time. I knew she had to, probably to follow her own sense of call. Sure, I had hoped she'd stay for 10 or 15 years—I've found that when the chemistry is right, longer pastorates can go deeper and lives can be touched more profoundly. But seven years was a pretty good tenure, and I'd heard good things of what Sarah was doing. People at other congregations had begun to talk about her as a "comer," so I wasn't surprised that she'd been snatched up. To be honest, I thought her leaving wasn't a bad thing at all. I felt confident that she had probably made a good choice even before I found out what she was going to do, and I felt confident that she'd be okay.

But I did feel for Al. A pastor's leaving is a big thing for someone who is a strong leader, who has responsibilities for the life of the congregation. It *does* feel like a train wreck. It *does* make you think panicky thoughts.

In the few minutes I had on the phone with Al I tried to cool him off and reminded him how they'd all felt when the previous pastor left. I told him how well Trinity had responded through the search that led to Sarah's call. And I told him about lots of other congregations going through similar dynamics. I don't know how much he heard—you really don't hear very well when your panic button has been pushed. But I also knew he was responding in a healthy way—looking for somebody to help, letting off some steam to somebody he trusted. In language I've learned to use—and will use with you—he was into finding directions. I felt confident that he'd make it, too.

I felt more than confident about the congregation! I really felt excited for them. Sure, they had difficult things to do in the months ahead; sure, their plans were in something of a cocked hat. But I knew that this was the very kind of disruption that had opened the door to constructive change for congregation after congregation that I had known or worked with.

I thought about what lay ahead for Trinity. They had a pretty good foundation—they had a good core of solid people, a mix of deeply committed Christians and others who were seekers or only partly committed. They gave to their church—some sacrificially. They had already made a real difference in the community with their after-school programs, their hospitality to AA and other groups. I knew they'd been key to the opening of a hospice in the area. They had a solid program to help adults grow in faith and church members had responsible roles in the life of the community and its business enterprises. They often fussed with their denomination about pronouncements from national boards and sometimes they grumbled about changes in the way things were done. They remembered with lots of pleasure many of the pastors who had preceded Sarah and sometimes repeated jokes that had been told in the pulpit years before. They remembered the jokes better than the sermons!

That's who they were. And I knew that they were entering something new. A time of transition and change. A time that seemed scary but that I knew was likely to be invigorating and downright exciting. They were going to learn new things about themselves and about their community and they were going to open new doors to the future.

I knew that because I'd seen dozens of congregations face the same kind of challenge. I knew most of them discovered they were on a journey to a new sense of their mission and to a new sense of themselves as a community. The folks at Trinity Church would spend time in the next months rethinking their basic values, learning anew what it meant to be followers of Jesus and builders of "church." They would explore their basic beliefs and take a new look at their assumptions. They would look at what earlier generations had said and meant

Trinity Church to be and they would have a chance to put their own stamp on what it was to become. They would probably also take a fresh look at their town—how *it* had changed. Indeed, they would have a chance to "own" the church that had been passed on to them by previous generations.

It's not inevitable, of course. I've known lots of congregations to face this change point and back away from it. They either are too afraid to take the risk of new life or they are too enamored of the status quo. They go through the motions or turn their life and their congregation's future over to somebody else who will "solve" their problem for them. I've known churches to grab up somebody really not equipped for the job just because they are handy, on the parish staff, or they live just down the road. If they do, they are refusing to take responsibility for their life. They miss a chance to explore God's call, a chance to grow. I get sad when I see that, but it happens.

I don't think I made all that clear to Al in that first phone call. Fortunately, later I had a chance to have more calls, and I think Al got a lot of what I meant.

Because this is a moment of extraordinary potential for a congregation, but because it is also a scary and sometimes difficult moment, this book is a chance for me to tell you why I was so hopeful for Al and Trinity Church. If you and your congregation are facing a moment like theirs—your pastor is leaving—this book really is a guide for you to the next months and to an exciting journey. If that's not where you are, don't worry. The time you spend reading this will not be wasted. My experience tells me that if that's not where you are now, you'll probably be there sometime in the next five to seven years, if not sooner.

Now, fasten your seat belt!

2

The Trip Ahead

OK—what else do I say to Al? He feels stuck in a problem and doesn't know what's to be done. I have reassured him that others have gone this way before and I've told him we know a lot about how to get from the resignation of a pastor to getting a new one. I'm not worried because I've seen it happen—but Al's in the position of most of the people in his congregation. Perhaps that's where you are, too.

In this book I plan to tell him (and you) what's ahead. But before we head into the journey, I need to clarify some of the dynamics that have suddenly come in to play.

Where we want to go is fairly clear—we want Al's congregation to pull itself together to seek a new pastor using the methods of his denomination and using the resources he can get. That's the destination. It's not unlike a family taking off for a trip together, say on vacation. *They* know the destination, too, but there are several ways to get there—and *how* they travel will make a big difference in how they feel when they get there. In the journey Al and his congregation are taking, there are several dynamics to which I want to point that will help get us there in one piece, ready for the vacation—and not spend a couple of days of hearing "Are we there yet?" from the back seat.

Trajectory of a Pastorate: The Purpose of the Journey

A key issue we need to look at is something we rarely think about—what I call the "trajectory" of a pastorate. When I first began to wrestle with what I call the "biography" of a pastorate—how it begins, grows, has its ups and downs, and finally comes to an end—I was working on the problem of whether it might be possible to work with clergy and laity in a congregation so that a strong, healthy relationship was generated—a relationship in which both the pastor and the congregation would be growing in their faith and in their ability to "do" congregation. It's easy to get a trajectory that moves upward at first; the enthusiasm of newness makes that almost inevitable. But I wanted a trajectory that didn't stall after a year or two—or worse, falter, slow down, and finally settle into a sliding-downward flat line.

Early on, it became clear to me that the quality of that relationship between the clergy and the laity was a key to the health and growth of the whole system. If that "connection" was a live one, it was like a lamp being plugged into a live electric circuit—the light would come on. If the connection was dead at either end, there would not be any light.

John Fletcher was a remarkable educator who in the 1970s conceived of a new kind of theological education based in local congregations, ecumenical and interfaith in nature. The seminary he founded, located in the Washington, D.C., metropolitan area, was called INTERMET. In order to plan that seminary's program, he decided to interview the people who were "consumers" of the product of theological seminaries—lay leaders in congregations who, as board members or in other leadership positions, "employed" clergy. The people he interviewed—well over a hundred of them—described a quality they valued most highly but that only emerged as the clergy and laity interacted over several years. He called that quality "religious authenticity." Interestingly, he discovered that the process by which religious authenticity develops requires interaction between the clergy and the laity of the congregation. The process he described was similar in many of the congregations, involving sequential, successively deeper challenges as the clergy and laity engaged with each other. Both pastor and congregation needed to be able to listen to each other and to be strong enough to confront each other. For my purposes, the key finding in his research was that, while the personal qualities of the pastor are important, religious authenticity only occurs *after* the pastor arrives as he or she enters into relationship with the congregation.[1]

That period of growing together, of interacting with one another, progressively learning from one another, is what I mean by "trajectory of ministry." The relationship retains a "liveness" to it. The question is, Are the clergy and laity able to be in the kind of dialogue that brings each to life? If so, religious authenticity may be possible.

That insight made me realize how faulty our thinking is about "finding a new pastor"—not only for Al and his congregation, but for your congregation as well. When Sarah Brookstone walked into Al Shepherdson's congregation some seven years before, she was only pastor in title and perhaps in church law. Al's voice on the telephone, however, told me that she had *become* the pastor in the years of living into the role. Not only that, the congregation had become a stronger center of ministry through its interaction with Sarah's leadership. Religious authenticity had been born in their dialogue. Sarah Brookstone and the congregation had experienced a pastorate that had a trajectory, that had taken off! Now they were facing its ending.

At this moment, the focus is not simply on the next pastor at Al's church, but on the trajectory of ministry that new pastor and the congregation will generate when he or she gets there. Will the new pastor (whoever he or she may be) be someone who can enter into an authentic relationship with the congregation rather than settle for being a plastic figure-head playing at being a religious leader? Will he not be so tender and sensitive that he cannot stand on his own feet in the face of difficulties or opposition? Can she grow into a real person with the people of this congregation? And the other side is equally important: can this congregation recover from the loss of Sarah and become even stronger, able to work with this new pastor, pushing him or her when they need to, going through tough times as well as happy ones, able to be party to real forgiveness when necessary?

You see, it's not about Al or Sarah or the new minister, it's about how all of them interact to make for a trajectory of ministry. The same is true for you and your congregation. It's not about the pastor who is leaving or the one who is coming. It's not even about you all who are stuck with having a lot of new jobs to do. It's about how you build from what has been the strength and integrity of one period of ministry into a new relationship in which a new ministry takes off for all of you.

If that building process really happens, the ministry will take off. If it does not happen, in a year or two you won't see a trajectory with pastor and people growing. Instead you will see a flat line, and probably both the pastor and the congregation wondering how to get out of a dead relationship. What I have observed—and it makes me sick every time I see it—is that too many pastorates just go dead like that. They kept breathing, but nobody grows and religious authenticity eludes both pastor and people. Often when that happens, the relationship deteriorates and pretty soon people start taking pot shots at each other or scapegoating one another.

My commitment has always been to help the trajectory take off in an upward direction. My faith is that if a live connection can get going between a pastor and a congregation, no matter how long or how short the pastorate is, that pastor will grow toward religious authenticity, and at the same time the congregation will deepen its life.[2]

So that's the first thing to look for. Yes, it's important to find a good pastor—the best a congregation can find. But it's even more important to find one in such a way that the pastor and the congregation increase in their ability to achieve a live connection in the years ahead.

I hope you are clear about wanting *more* than a pastor—that you want to work at increasing the potential for a pastor-people dialogue where both grow in authenticity. That has to do with the *purpose of the journey*.

Procedures and Processes

Procedures are the things we have to do to make the journey come off—just the sheer nuts and bolts of it, such as deciding to drive rather than take a plane or train. Then, if that is the decision, getting the car fixed up for the journey; deciding how and what to pack; choosing the route and the stopping places. On the journey to get a new pastor we have learned a lot of the stopping places and alternative routes that are out there—the advantages and disadvantages of taking either the scenic routes or the direct routes. We need a map of that journey and a tour guide for reference. I'll call that "the map of the territory."

Think about a memorable vacation you have taken with your family. Do you remember trying to tell friends why the trip was so great? It is frustrating. You can pull out the map and talk about the distance from here to there. You can point to the scary mountain road and tell about the terrible storm you met. But the listener's eyes glaze over when you start talking about things that made all the difference in building your family memories. Even the photographs you took don't carry the impact. So much that happened isn't in the pictures, isn't on the map. The relationships that shape the success of a vacation are often helped or hurt by how you deal with all the stuff that happens: packing the car, spending a day or two jammed in together, and the resulting emotional climate (from enjoying one another to smoldering resentment and long-held grudges). How you deal with frustrations or surprises (the drawbridge that stays open too long, the memorably awful meal at a stopover). The way one person tries to control everything and another plays games of "getting even." The wild moments of giggling about nothing at all. The family jokes that get invented in the middle of boredom. The games of cow poker or contests to find the most state license plates. I guess I don't have to hint at many other examples to remind you that what happens on vacation can often be vastly helped or hurt by what goes on during the journey you take to get to your destination.

I have a friend who talks about that as the "horizontal" dimension of a trip—the stuff you see on a map. She goes on to point to the "vertical" dimension of a trip—the moments of encountering something very deep or something very high, the moments of awe, of beauty, or of fear. You can describe the things on the horizontal journey, take photographs of them. But the things of the vertical journey are too deep, too touching, too overwhelming to be communicated.

In addition to the physical, horizontal dimension, I want to point to that second, vertical dimension of our journey. Not the "procedures" for getting there but the "processes" you need to watch all through the journey to help make the vacation all it can be. The procedures are the maps and instructions. The processes are the things that happen that make the vacation something to sit at home and reminisce about: "Remember the time Joe fell into the creek?" "Remember those *awful* pancakes Dad cooked in the hamburger fat?" "Remember watching the sun go down from the motel balcony?"

Those are memories of processes that happen. The human response to such memorable occurrences is to try to set down the procedures that make them happen. Well, procedures don't make processes happen. They *can* help you avoid dead ends; they *can* put you on the best road. But no procedure will *make* good processes happen.

We do have a map of the key procedure areas. There are seven stopovers that will inevitably occur between the time Al phoned me about—when the pastor announces her resignation—and the end of the journey when a new pastor is in place at the heart of Al's congregation. These are the same stopovers you will experience in your journey to find the right pastor. This will be a valuable guide, just like the map you took on that vacation.

But the list of stopovers on that map may be second in importance to the "Process List"—a second map that outlines the developmental issues which will be on the agenda to be worked on all the time you are on that journey. Perhaps it's not a second map but an overlay of the first.

The first map tells you where you are going and helps you organize for the tasks—"pack the car!" The second map of the processes is the one that will lead to growth and change, and will be the one most likely to produce the memories and stories that will enrich the congregation for years to come.

Here are the stopovers on the map of the territory, the *procedures*. They occur sequentially. I will take them apart in chapter 3:

1. Termination (one pastor leaves)
2. Direction finding (the congregation chooses its path)
3. Self-study (finding out who and where the congregation is)
4. Search (looking for the "right" pastor)

5. Decision/Negotiation (making a decision and reaching agreements)
6. Installation (getting the new pastor on the job)
7. Start-up (beginning to build a new ministry in the congregation and the community

Here are the *process* issues you will deal with on the journey. They are not sequential but keep occurring and reoccurring as the journey goes on. I have come to call them the "developmental tasks." This is the "process map" I will discuss in chapter 4:

1. Coming to terms with the congregation's history
2. Discovering a new identity, a new sense of mission
3. Helping the congregation's internal leadership to grow and change
4. Rediscovering linkages to the denomination
5. Establishing a new commitment between people and the new pastor to engage in their mission together

Look at the procedures and processes as a matrix:

		Developmental Tasks				
		Task 1	Task 2	Task 3	Task 4	Task 5
	Step 1: Termination	x	x	x	x	x
	Step 2: Direction Finding	x	x	x	x	x
	Step 3: Self-Study	x	x	x	x	x
Sequential Tasks	Step 4: Search	x	x	x	x	x
	Step 5: Decision/Negotiation	x	x	x	x	x
	Step 6: Installation	x	x	x	x	x
	Step 7: Start-up	x	x	x	x	x

At every step of the procedures, *all* of the developmental tasks or processes are in play. Some processes are engaged more heavily in earlier or later steps, but every step gives opportunity to attend to all processes. The key is to keep all the processes in mind through all the steps. What cannot be completed early can be addressed in later steps.

Al's congregation in Oklahoma City will take all seven of the steps on the map, no question. Our systems are set up to be sure that will happen. It will also be so for you.

The only question is the quality with which those steps will be taken. It is quite possible to come to the end and hire a new pastor, and that's it. A new hired hand takes over to do the chores of pastoral leadership. If he or she is unusually gifted, some really great things may happen. If he or she is not very gifted, the congregation is likely go into stagnation or simply into depression.

If, however, during this period the congregation and its leaders keep focused on the developmental tasks, there is a possibility that much better things can happen. Instead of hiring a new hand, the congregation and the new pastor may discover a brand-new call from each other. What could be born is the kind of creative relationship between people and pastor in which both become more than they had ever been before. What could be born is a new, challenging community with a new lay and clergy leadership team ready to open up new pages of mission together. There can be born a lively relationship in which pastor *and* people continually call each other deeper, to stronger ministry.

Another way of saying that is that the trajectory of ministry is more likely to take off if you pay attention to these processes as you go on the journey. Indeed, you may want to slow down our journey on the map to be sure you are taking enough time for the developmental steps.

All of that is what I knew and that's why I tried to encourage Al. Yes, the loss of a pastor can be difficult for any congregation. Yes, they will have a time of uncertainty and change. But the bottom line is measured in the potential of this moment. Indeed, there is no more critical moment in the life of a congregation than this moment in which it faces going from one pastoral leader to another.

If that is where your congregation is, then hang on for the time of your life. Yes, you have a challenge ahead of you, but this may be a challenge that can make this one of the most memorable journeys you've ever taken.

3

Steps Along the Journey

We begin the journey. Experience tells us it will take some time. The time between one pastor's leaving and the next one's installation can vary—I have known it to be as short as six months or as long as two years. My general assessment is that if it takes less than 12 months, there isn't much time to take care of the qualitative issues—the developmental tasks. If it takes more than 18 months you may run into leadership overload or depression. Having an interim pastor around to manage the day-to-day work of the congregation can relieve the parish leadership team so they don't get overloaded. Having consultative help for the search committee can help them do a better job and not waste time doing it.

It is important to know this because almost all congregations have a strong subgroup that puts on a lot of pressure for quick action. Those people are not necessarily your friends. That pressure for quick action needs to be heard but not heeded. Yes, you *can* act quickly—there are pastors out there eager for a job. But it is like the married person suddenly widowed—sure, there are possible matches out there, but many of the hasty marriages formed at such a time result in plenty of regrets and miserable matches. "Marry in haste: repent at leisure"—the old saying is worth paying attention to.

Much of the pressure for going out and getting a pastor right away is based on some serious fallacies. Some people say, "We've got to get a new pastor in right away so the whole place doesn't go to pot." That represents a clergy-centered understanding of ministry that doesn't reflect the theological consensus in many denominations that ministry really is based in both clergy and laity. This sort of statement indicates a real put-down of the leadership and effectiveness of the laity who form the heart of the congregation.

Not only that—it's *wrong*. The place *won't* go to pot. In case after case strong laity rise to the occasion and bring new strength to a congregation during these trying months. Many congregations come to look back on this time of pastoral exploration and search as one of remarkable growth in many ways.

This congregational pressure for immediate action is sometimes based on a mechanistic idea of change. This view holds that pastors are interchangeable and that one can be replaced by another as you would switch bulbs in a lamp. If you think that way, go ahead and try it. My experience is that pastoral change is a deeply human interaction and process. The leaving of one pastor opens deep dimensions of grief in a congregation and the installation of another requires touching equally deep emotions of new relationship.

An early Alban Institute monograph on this time in a parish's life was called *Prime Time for Renewal*, just to make that very point.[1] The period between pastors is a time of growth and development that can lead to a much stronger congregation—if the time is taken to do the work well.

Let's get on the journey, then.

Step One: Termination of One Pastor

The termination of a pastor's ministry in one place is more than an event; it is really a process that may cover a number of months.

Think for a moment about the case I have been referring to, that of Al Shepherdson's pastor, Sarah Brookstone, in the Trinity Church congregation in Oklahoma City. I had last been in touch with them seven years earlier when Sarah began her pastorate. All I had heard on the grapevine was that she was doing a good job—friends in the congregation reported that she had been elected to the board of her regional denomination, she had survived a battle when she reoriented the music program, and she and the board had done a good job of undergirding the operating finances of the congregation. From outside the congregation I heard that she had been invited to teach a summer continuing education course at her seminary and was becoming known as a very able preacher.

Not a bad "trajectory," one might think. Just the kind of trajectory that would do two things at once: (1) call her to the attention of congregations and leaders in the church who might be looking for new leadership and (2) make Sarah aware of other possibilities for her future and raise the question of how best to use her skills for the church. I would guess that for the past year or two people had been dropping hints to Sarah to see if she was "ready" to move on or if she was "open" to a call to another challenge. And from time to time she heard the hints.

The stage of "termination" often starts like this: it begins with the pastor fully intending to stay and gradually passes to a time in which other possibilities come along and are resisted. Finally an offer arrives that the pastor cannot refuse.

In my experience that's the usual way termination happens. Occasionally it is a bolt out of the blue, but usually the pastor has felt the stirrings for some time, and often the congregation has begun to have hints that the pastor may be "in play." I've known congregations to become so anxious about this that the pastors have to defend themselves any time they take a weekend off. And I still remember the calling committee that came to see me in my first pastorate—committee members dressed very conservatively, rented a black Ford, and tried to be very inconspicuous (in a parish with 40 persons in the service). They did not know that by the time the car had gotten to the church the phones were ringing all over town: "Who are those four people going to our church in that black Ford?"

Signals get sent and received. It was healthy that Sarah had grown in her ministry to the point that she began to see other options. It was also healthy that a number of people felt connected to her and did not want her to leave.

I bring this up because the way the weeks are spent between Sarah's decision to leave and her actual departure will affect the ministry of the next pastor.[2] And generally there is nobody who feels responsible for this time—probably no search committee or pastor-seeking committee is in place yet.

If anyone is to manage this time, it probably has to be the congregation's board (session, vestry, or council). Four tasks stand out as needing attention at this point:

1. *Clarifying and organizing the time before the current pastor leaves.* Sometimes it is hard to pin down specific dates— there may be real estate issues that affect the pastor's departure date; there may be issues of terminal financial pay and of unused vacation; somebody needs to make decisions about a parish "gift." None of these things is monumental, but somebody needs to see that they are taken care of. It's rarely clear who that is.

2. *Organizing an event or set of events for "saying goodbye."* There should be some "public" events, depending on the style of the congregation and how the community has been involved in the pastorate. There also should be adequate time saved for the pastor to be able to have times in smaller groups for speaking more personally with some people.

3. *Supporting the pastor, who is likely to be going through a lot of stress and may not be very clear or good about decision mak-*

ing during this time. There are three particular areas in which a pastor's decision making is often colored by his or her anxiety: (*a*) when to leave (often the emotional pull is to stay too long); (*b*) how to influence the future pastorate (this is not the "old" pastor's business and he or she needs to be told forcefully to bug off); and (*c*) what kind of public events are needed for the "goodbyes" (the pastor's modesty or lack of it is not the issue—this is something the congregation needs to do even if the pastor is reluctant—it can be called false modesty).

4. *Reassuring the members of the congregation that everything is under control* (even if you're not positive that it is!). Congregations that lose their pastors can get panicky. That doesn't help anybody.

There are also "special cases" of termination that need to be noted.

1. *Termination after very long pastoral tenures.* If the former pastor has been around a relatively long time (sometimes as few as eight years, sometimes as many as 25), you can expect some issues to surface. There may be an effort to crown one of the associates with the senior pastor's position. Don't listen to stuff about "Elijah's mantle for Elisha"—you can't expect a fiery chariot to fix this one! This has been known to work, but it is almost always an unhappy choice, both for the person chosen and for the congregation. This is one of the situations in which the use of a trained interim pastor for a year or more is strongly recommend. A similar dynamic is present in congregations with large staffs—there may be parties in the congregation supporting different staff members to be chosen pastor. The use of an interim pastor is always preferable to choosing one of the associates. For one thing, it "protects" the associate who may want to consider staying on in the next pastorate. If the associate is interim and is not selected as senior pastor, the new pastor almost always has to let the associate go. If the associate *is* selected as pastor, everyone

may lose—the congregation has avoided a chance to make a choice for the future, and the associate may never be accepted as the senior pastor.

After such a long pastorate lay leaders are often reluctant to be direct and clear with the pastor who has served them so long and for whom they have very warm feelings. Interim pastors are sometimes able to speak more directly about things that really have to be said or clarified ("What day are you actually moving out of the pastor's residence—we have to get it painted!" or "Where is the checkbook for the outreach committee?").

2. *Termination for Retirement.* Pastors approaching retirement frequently have several things going on that make decision making murky and difficult for their congregations. Sometimes they need extra working time to qualify for pension benefits; sometimes they have such commitments to the lives of their congregations that they waffle every time they think about leaving, sending confusing signals. Sometimes they are so anxious about what they will do after retirement that they cannot make up their minds. In these situations, the church board or its head needs to take responsibility to push for a certain date. However, they should call in career-assessment people or consultants, pension-fund people, church executives and bishops, who can help them negotiate the close of the pastorate. One must avoid at all costs the kind of delayed action that says, "Well, I'll leave at the first of this year, take a sabbatical, and then come back next Christmas and retire." It is important that when the pastor leaves it means leaving the position and the legal authority, otherwise the hands of the search committee are tied and neither the work of termination can be done nor can the search process begin. Most pension groups will permit continuing to pay the pastor toward the pension while vacating the position. I've suggested to some the use of the term "terminal sabbatical,"

meaning they have left the position completely, but that they will be having a period of paid leave afterwards. It is probably not wise to give the retiring pastor a title (pastor emeritus or something like that) until several years after he or she leaves. An interim pastor worth his or her salt can walk in and be direct in sorting some of this out even when members of the congregation are gun-shy.

3. *Termination after Pastoral Trauma—Firing or Misbehavior.* I am speaking of two kinds of pastoral trauma not because they are at all the same thing but because both leave such emotional and institutional wreckage behind. In the case of the firing of the pastor (or a forced resignation) you always are dealing with "winners" and "losers" of a strong conflict. In the case of a firing for misbehavior you have those dynamics *plus* even deeper emotional wounds. In both cases you are probably dealing with issues of secrecy and loss of trust across the board. Again, this is a time and place for an experienced, trained interim pastor. Many times it is also important to use psychotherapeutic assistance to help the congregation cope with its trauma.[3]

Step one on our map of the territory of pastoral change ends when the pastor and the pastor's family pack up and leave. This step happens inevitably. I have pointed to some of the hiccoughs and glitches that can happen along the way. How this step is taken can help both the pastor and the congregation to be stronger in their next pastorates.

Sarah is going to leave Oklahoma City. Will the way she leaves and how the congregation helps it happen strengthen the congregation for the future, or will it leave so many unfinished pieces of business that the first year or two of the next pastorate will be spent sweeping up the debris? And will that happen to your congregation as you begin to lead it toward choosing your next pastor? That's our primary concern. The answer to that question? It all depends.

A secondary concern: will the way Sarah (or your pastor) leaves help her enter new relationships unencumbered by personal unfinished business? That depends, too.

Step Two: Direction Finding

Even before the pastor packs and leaves, the congregation—especially its leaders—enters the stage of direction finding. Reading this book may be part of your direction finding.

Most denominational systems have sets of procedures and protocols to advise congregations on how to go about seeking another pastor. One peculiarity in congregational life is that nobody seems to remember what those procedures are. No matter how recently the congregation may have gone through a pastoral search, everyone seems to have forgotten what that entails—even the ones who served on the earlier committees.

Confusion abounds. Loud voices also abound—often voices of people who are trying to seize control. One of the first voices Al will hear at his next board or committee meeting is someone saying, "Oh, this is no problem. We replace personnel all the time in our company, and we have a fail-safe method for doing it." Note that voice but don't turn the process over to him or her—the processes used in business and management are enormously helpful in church life, and you may well want that person's assistance at some point. But not at the beginning. Think twice about putting that person on the search committee—he or she may hijack it, like a congregation I heard about that used a personnel manual from a mass-market restaurant to find a new pastor.

Regardless of how close or distant you have been from your denomination's regional office (presbytery, diocese, conference, synod, or whatever they call that office), there will be people there who know the ropes, who know the recommended steps, and who have dealt with pastoral changes many, many times. They can help you avoid all sorts of dead ends. Many of the denominations have procedures they recommend or, in other cases, requirements that you ignore at your peril. Additionally, many of them have resources they can make available to you, including access to names and dossiers of consultants, interim pastors, and pastoral candidates. None of them will solve your problems. Most of them can help. Usually they have a very high stake in your securing absolutely the best candidate for your pastorate. They want you to succeed!

You do not, usually, have to follow their advice blindly; however, knowing what they know is a distinct advantage if you decide to bend some of the rules. As you gather information from them you can assess how helpful they can be, locating the one or two people you may want to keep in touch with in case of future difficulty. If it's possible, have one or two members of the committee go to the regional office to make a personal connection. You may also want to invite one or two people from the regional office to visit with your board to give them an orientation and to respond to questions. Often it is also helpful during this direction-finding time to connect with one or two congregations nearby who recently did a search to find out what they did and why—as well as what they'd do differently if they had a chance!

This part of the map comes to the end with the establishment of a search committee. Here are some of the things you need to be clear about and have board agreement on by the time the search committee is set up. Sometimes some of this is negotiated between the search committee and the board in a joint meeting early in the process:

a. What size should the search committee be and who should be on it?

b. Is there to be an interim pastor (generally decided by the board and responsible to them) and what is his/her relationship to the search committee?

c. Is the search committee free to secure its own consultant?

d. What is the budget for the search committee?

e. What is expected of the search committee (i.e., present one name? Several names?)?

f. What is the timeline both the board and the committee can agree on?

g. What does the regional office have as resources and requirements (e.g., can they do background checks on candidates? Is it required that they see the candidate list ahead of time? Do they have suggested norms for the relationship between the search committee and the board? How does the search committee access denominationally recommended candidates?)?

One troublesome point: almost every pastoral search goes beyond the dates of congregational elections. Several new board members will likely get elected in the middle of the search. Early on, the board and search committee have worked hard to clarify a lot of things, but when new board members are elected, they are unaware of the previous agreements. Both the board and the search committee need to pay attention to that moment—some say one ought to consider that a change in board membership really constitutes a brand-new board. The board may not be terribly conscious of this difference, but the search committee that ignores it can get in deep trouble. The two groups need to be sure that the new board is really on board with what had been agreed upon by the earlier group.

Step Three: Self-Study

I deliberately put this step next, and I want to tell you why I do it this way. The next two *tasks* are "self-study" and "search." They are quite different tasks, and I believe it is important to do them sequentially so the first can modify what is done in the second. There are people who try to do the two tasks at the same time, often subdividing the search committee into one subcommittee to do the self-study and another to begin the search. Such an allocation of tasks can do two things that are highly popular: (1) shorten the time between pastors by between two and four months, and (2) respond to the heavy anxiety in the congregation to "start getting the names" of potential candidates.

The *point* of doing the self-study is to clarify what kind of leader the congregation is likely to need. The self-study is intended to look at the congregation and its community and develop the directions of ministry that seem to be calling the congregation. In a sense the self-study tries to discern what the "job description" of the parish is for the next few years of its ministry. It is from that job description that the search committee can begin to identify the characteristics and skills they need for the clergyperson who best can lead in that direction. The self-study should drive the search.

When the two tasks are done simultaneously it is unlikely that the self-study will affect what kinds of candidates go on the list the search committee is collecting. Such a search can turn out to be a "beauty contest" trying to identify the most winsome personality among the possible candidates. What we *want* to do is to see that the self-study is translated into the criteria of leadership that can fit *this* congregation *now*.

Let's look at self-study, then, assuming it to be a task to be carried out before you focus on looking for candidates. (If there is a lot of anxiety about names, set up a good filing system and let people send names in. Just don't start processing any of it until the self-study is well along.)

Self-studies go on all the time in congregations. Usually they are done casually and without much discipline. You hear the outcomes of self-studies when you hear people saying things like: "Well, we've had two pastors in a row from XXX Seminary. I think we ought to try graduates of YYY Seminary—I think their biblical studies are better." "The pastor who's leaving has been a terrible administrator—we must have better management now that the budget is larger." "We're in such a slump of membership and money—we need a real 'go-getter' who'll fill the pews and the coffers." "We need to get a more traditionalist approach." "We need somebody to appeal to the young people the way the parish used to." Such self-study sometimes represents feelings of several members, sometimes it is the idiosyncratic comment of one person. Be careful: sometimes very loud people are speaking only for themselves, and they can be dead wrong.

I am sure a case could be made that such comments may each have some merit, but they represent a very limited viewpoint. What's needed is not to ignore such comments, but to build a way to get a broader picture and to begin to see what it is in the community that is calling out for the ministry of this congregation. That is what self-study is all about.

How congregations go about this task varies enormously. In some cases three or four of the "old timers" prop their feet up on the table in somebody's back office, reminisce about the good old days, and decide what kind of a pastor they need "nowadays." It is easy to debunk this approach, but I have to admit that once or twice I have seen this work quite well— some of those "old timers" are remarkably perceptive as to what was and what has come to pass.

Other congregations develop elaborate schemes for data collection and analysis. I have seen genuinely professional studies turned out by such committees, although I have also seen committees overwhelmed by the volume of data their excitement led them to accumulate. Data overload is a constant temptation. If you use an interim consultant (see chapter 5), that person will have some options for you.

An area often overlooked is data about the community in which the congregation resides—what the trends are in demographics, what is happening to the economic base, what kinds of people are coming in or going out, what age groups dominate.

I always look for a combination of hard statistical information and lots of anecdotal perception. I do look out for (and try not to get seduced by) the statistical whiz kid in the congregation who tends to overwhelm people with the sophistication of the data. The denominational office will be able to put you in touch with people who can give you elaborate studies of the geographic area contiguous to your congregation. If they send you such studies, be sure they also provide someone who can help you interpret and use the material they send.

Self-studies move toward some sort of document, sometimes called a parish profile. Such a document is intended to be a description of what the congregation has discovered about itself, its strengths and its weaknesses. An important part of the self-study comes as the data is collected and before the profile is written, however, by having the congregation react to the data. Again, there are dozens of ways to have that happen. Send a draft in the mail and ask for feedback (that will give everybody a voice); have a series of meetings in members' homes to read and discuss the profile, with someone recording responses; use the profile as the basis for several weeks of Sunday adult forums.

The point is not to get precision but to get involvement and engagement as the congregation tries to think what kind of leadership it is going to need. This is to help the congregation get clearer about what challenges lie ahead and to begin to get connected to those challenges even before the new pastor is selected.

After the congregation has provided feedback, the search committee then can produce a document. If the job leading up to this step is well done, many people of the congregation will already be on board with the kind of leadership they will probably need and won't have a lot more need for the document. However, the potential candidates and the people who want to suggest candidates will be greatly helped by the document.

The profile Al Shepherdson's congregation will come up with *after* Sarah Brookstone leaves will probably be substantially different from the profile that preceded her coming. Both the community and the congregation will have experienced change in Sarah's years of tenure, and the challenge for leadership will be different.

Step Four: Search

The search is the most easily understood step in seeking to change pastors. It is also a very complex operation requiring very astute information management and strict confidentiality on the part of the committee. By now you will want to have set up a secure place where personnel records can be kept and where committee members *only* have access as needed.

The upside-down pyramid on the next page illustrates what happens:

At point 1, you will have received over-the-transom dossiers, nominations, and names. You will have a number of names and thin or almost nonexistent details about any of them. How many names you have will vary with the supply of clergy, the vitality and challenge of the pastoral situation, and the vigor with which you have sought out potential names.

1. XXXXXXXXXXXXXXXXXXXXXXXXXXXXXXXXXXXXXXXX
(Many candidates, inconsistent data)

2. XXXXXXXXXXXXXXXXXXXXXXXXXXXXXX
(Obviously unqualified dropped;
better data on those left)

3. XXXXXXXXXXXXXXXXX
(Follow-up data sought; references
checked; some stand-out
candidates begin to emerge)

4. XXXXXXXX
(Search committee teams
visit handful of high-
potential candidates)

5. XXX
(Several "finalists"
visit the congregation;
interviews;
selection of the
nominee for
board action)

6. X
(Call issued
and accepted)

Be sure to invite members of the congregation to make nominations. Some come in with little or no urging. Others—many of them the best qualified and most well trained—will be reluctant even to have their names listed. Your job is to push those people to be part of the process.

The problem of the pyramid becomes evident here. You *cannot* keep all names under consideration—but *by what criteria* do you cull any of them out?

The "cut" that occurs first, leaving you at point 2, is almost entirely based on what you have received up to now:

paper. This process generates lots of paper, and you need to have a secure way to keep files where committee members can have access but others cannot. You will need to spend time making sure that people get thanked for the names they sent in and, if that name is turned down later on, they should hear of its disposition.

The information is not very deep at first and somewhat inconsistent. Some names are clearly unsuitable for the particular situation, but the committee will have to use the profile to discover criteria for determining who are the obvious misfits and who are the ones who just as obviously need to be kept. At this point the search committee needs to seek supplementary paper information; sometimes the denomination will have personnel dossiers in which the information is somewhat similar but in a more standardized format. Every step of the way it gets more important to have good filing and record systems going. Some congregations hire a part-time secretary for this task. Getting as many of those "standardized" dossiers as possible makes comparisons much easier, although it must be remembered that most of what is in the dossier is material supplied by the candidate. Be sure your capacity to receive and use electronic data is secure—you want committee members and no one else to have access to these files, and you want to avoid potential corruption by computer viruses.

By position 3 on the chart, you will begin going deeper into information about each candidate. You will start asking for (or telephoning for) information from the listed references or other people you know who know the candidate. By this time you will also have massaged the profile enough to have a much clearer sense of the set of qualifications you are looking for and a small group of outstanding candidates will begin to appear. Do not be surprised, however, if some who look outstanding at this point slip out of contention later.

Also, some who do not look outstanding yet may show surprising strength later. Be open to what is happening.

At almost any point in the process you may become privy to information that must be maintained in confidentiality. You will want to have a clear expectation that all members will refrain from public comment on matters the committee discusses. You may have to arrange for confidential data gathering by a third party. Denominational officers and your search consultant can supplement you here.

At position 4 you will be sending small groups of the search committee to visit the congregations where you can get some first-hand knowledge of the candidates and how their ministry is carried out in the other congregation. Your teams for visiting need to be carefully selected and trained. All through the pyramid you will find consultants very helpful if they are available to you, but especially in these last few levels of the pyramid. Sometimes the decisions to drop or keep a name are very difficult—consultants can provide more complex kinds of "voting" methods to test not only the most desired candidate and the least desired candidate, but also the candidate with fewer strongly opposed committee members. The committee may need to look at such votes when the decisions get difficult. Another step (position 5) that many, though not all, congregations take is to invite three or four of the most promising candidates to visit the congregation and have an informal visit with a group of leaders—this gives the search committee an opportunity to bring a wider sample of leadership opinion in an advisory capacity and gives a reality check to the committee's perceptions.

At position 6 you make your selection and communicate it to the board.

Throughout this time and for the rest of the pastoral change process, it is critical to keep the board abreast of where the search committee is and what it is doing. If a member of the board serves on the search committee, some of that will take care of itself. But the search committee probably will want to plan to place regular reports in the parish newsletter or on a bulletin board. One should stay away from details ("we have 43 people on our list and have dropped 14") in favor of general information. ("We are working with the parish profile to review the large number of persons who have been recommended to us. We hope to be able to visit a few of the leading candidates by two months from now. Our goal is still to be able to nominate a candidate by January 1, but holidays may put us a month later. We will keep you informed.")

Confidentiality becomes more and more critical—even with the board. Premature "leaks" can be damaging to continuing negotiations as well as to the candidates under consideration.

Step Five: Decision/Negotiation

The double name of this step gives evidence of the fact that things get tense and interconnected as you get closer to the end of the journey to a new pastor. These two actions of decision and negotiation interpenetrate one another for quite some time. It is possible for this to muddy things up—a good consultant can help keep the action clear.

You see, the decision about the "right" candidate actually begins the first time the committee decides to drop a name from the list of active prospects. It occurs months before the final decision. And as the committee moves through its life and their actions move "down" the pyramid, dozens of decisions are made. Each one helps clarify what it understands the self-study to mean and how the group defines the kind of leadership it is looking for. These decisions are negative decisions: By saying "no" to this or these candidates we are saying "yes" to others and to another direction. We are not focusing on the person of the candidates, we are focusing on decisions about the direction the self-study tells us we are called to go. The better the committee is at working this tension, learning to say no to some and yes to others, the finer they are tuning their sense of what God is calling their congregation to be and do in this generation.

The final decision they reach, to present one candidate as their nominee to the board or to the congregation, is simply a refinement of what they have been doing for several months. One shouldn't deny, however, that the final decisions get harder and harder. As one goes down the pyramid one's personal investment in and knowledge of the candidates goes up. By the final decisions between three or four candidates, you will be choosing between people you have come to know and honor and, in many cases, to love! Again, I will only note that it often helps to have a consultant to help referee the final decisions!

One question deserves special note: does the search committee present one name or several? It is my experience that it is best to present a single name to the committee or group that makes the final decision. That does require, however, working hard to be sure the trust between the searchers and the final deciders is kept high. This is difficult if there is strong polarization within the congregation and board. It is hard, but it can be done, and it requires complex decision making beyond an "up and down" vote. A consultant can help design a process (mentioned above) in which rather than choosing a "winner" and a "loser," you try to determine which candidate attracts less antagonism, which is more likely a candidate the extremes can accept. If several names are given, it is all too likely that the board will have to redo the search itself. And it may be more difficult for the board, in a more political situation, to find middle ground if that is necessary.

Negotiation accompanies decision making and similarly spreads itself over some considerable time. Some negotiation may occur between the board and the committee, such as over whether to have a regional or a national search.

Most congregations enter into a contract with their pastors. Be clear about who and how that contract will be negotiated before it's time to do it. Ask your bishop, executive, or staffperson for samples of contracts used in other congregations. If it is appropriate, ask the staffperson to assist in developing the contract. The search committee members will want to be sure that the final contract reflects the directions and intentions discovered in the self-study.

Because the search committee members will make visits to some of the candidates and some of the candidates will be visiting the congregation, it is crucial for the search committee to know some of the parameters of what they can discuss with the candidates. The candidates need to know some things they can factor into their own decisions: something of the expectations of budget support and salary, something of the living quarters the congregation plans to make available, or the amount it will pay for. The search committee needs to have some general parameters it can use in its conversations, but it also needs to be clear about who is in charge of the final negotiations. Clear communication between the search committee and the board can save a lot of grief.

Step Six: Installation

The selection of a new pastor is a significant moment in the life of a congregation. It is a time to pull out the stops and whistles internally in the congregation but also in the ecumenical and interfaith community. The board needs to set up a committee to focus on this as an event, or perhaps as several events.

I have a large prejudice that the central acts of the installation should be in the context of worship—worship that reflects the best of the congregation's tradition, yes, but that also moves into some of what the parish profile talked about as the future call of the congregation. This is an occasion for celebrating the new image this congregation wants to live into.

There are other mundane issues about installation. Beforehand, you need to be sure that the family arrangements are clear, that living space is ready, that equipment the new pastor will need is in place. If the pastor has children, assistance with school arrangements needs to be offered (which requires particular care if they move in the summer and the children have no community of school for several months). The congregation should also assist the pastor's spouse if he or she needs to make connections for jobs or appointments.

Step Seven: Start-up

Some may find it confusing even to *have* a step seven, since it refers to a time *after* the new pastor has arrived! Installation is understandable, because it is a kind of "end game" for our subject. Some years ago, however, while congregational researchers like myself were wrestling with the whole system of pastoral change, it became clear that what has come to be called "start-up" is the forgotten part of the system. When the pastor is in place, the search committee has a party and retires. The bishop, executive, or staffperson crosses one more parish placement off the calendar.

Yet that is precisely the point at which a new kind of energy needs to be invested in strengthening the pastorate. So much energy has been invested, perhaps for a year or even two, to sorting out the future the parish feels called to, to clarifying what kind of leadership is needed, to searching for and recruiting that leadership—and now everybody assumes all is well.

The fact is that when the new pastor is on the scene the time has come to activate the dreams, build the relationships, set the framework for productive working together. If that work of activation is done well, the pastor will *be* in a live connection with the laity, a pastor-lay leadership team will be developing, and the scene will be set for a decade or two of creative learning and working.

Not every pastor comes equipped to initiate that new teamwork, however. Not every congregation that *asks* for new leadership really *wants* it when they discover the new leader wants to go ways they had not bargained for. In short, when reality sets in, a lot of potentially tremendous clergy and lay leaders can easily get crosswise with one another. And it is in the first year that the relationship can become very strong— or irreparably damaged.

This is not the burden of this book. But I would be remiss if I did not alert pastors and congregations who have struggled to find each other that finding each other does not take the place of learning to work in the new relationship. It is a risky business, mistakes are going to be made, false starts are going to occur, and strong teams of leaders need to be built in order for congregations to recover and make new starts.

Several important books by Roy Oswald illuminate what can be done,[4] but we are also fortunate that several of the denominational systems have begun programs like "First Start" in the ELCA and "Fresh Start" in the Episcopal Church, and several theological seminaries, stimulated by Lilly Endowment grants, are strengthening their work for seminary graduates in the first few years out. All of these will build the skill-set of our newer clergy to be better at starting a new piece of work.

My point is to put this start-up step on the agenda of every congregation that seeks and gets a new pastor, to remind them that there is work to do when the new pastor arrives. The work has to do with making dreams and plans become flesh and blood. It involves building teams of clergy and laity committed to actualizing new directions in mission and ministry.

Getting a new pastor is important, and that has been your task through step six. Don't forget the critical importance of step seven in the enthusiasm of having completed the search. Step seven is when your joint ministry gets started.

4

The Terrain and the Climate of the Journey

The chart at the end of chapter 2 (p. 18) underlies this chapter and its predecessor. Chapter 3 describes the sequential steps of the task ahead. In this chapter I will be focused on the nonsequential developmental tasks, the processes that need to happen during the journey. Chapter 3 describes the horizontal journey; this chapter describes the vertical journey.

Here the focus will be on the five developmental tasks congregations will not always do, or at least will not always do well. The procedures, the sequential steps, have to happen, but these tasks do not. If they are not done, however, it will affect enormously the quality of the ministry that comes out at the other end. Now I want to show how those steps form a framework within which the developmental tasks can happen.

Here, then, are brief descriptions of the five tasks that are central to bringing about the kind of new relationship between pastor and people that Al Shepherdson's congregation and yours want to foster.

The First Developmental Task:
Coming to Terms with the Past

Every congregation lives in dialogue with its past. Every congregation is strengthened immeasurably by its history, but every congregation has also been deeply wounded by its past. It is both the heir and the victim of its story.

Congregations are not blank slates simply waiting for a new pastor to write a totally new story. A pastor sometimes is confused by resistance to what he or she plans to do in "their" congregation. The congregation is a living, breathing cauldron of ministry and story and mission and tragedy. It is not waiting for the pastor to bring life—life is already there and they are living a ministry that was there before their recent pastor and it will be there when the new pastor is long gone.

There are two extremes I've observed in pastor placement—extremes I think to be pathological, extremes I think the entire search process is intended to help us escape.

At one end of this scale the pastoral placement is a hostile takeover. The pastoral candidate has such a strong commitment (to a management style, to a theological approach, to an understanding of religious community) that he or she comes in to wipe out the past and start all over. In such a placement the new pastor often flushes out all remnants of the previous patterns of the congregation and imposes his or her own imprint upon it. The past is eliminated. Usually many members of the congregation leave—sometimes immediately, in other cases over a year or two. (Healthier congregations throw the fool out!)

I see such an outcome as badly flawed. It comes from the assumption that the pastor "owns" the ministry and "is" the ministry. It assumes that the people of the congregation are not intrinsic to the ministry. (I remember an Army chaplain's comment when I asked him how he managed to move to a new place and initiate a new work every three years, which was then the standard in the chaplaincy: "Easy—I assume they never had ministry until I got there.") All too many clergy I know have assumptions not unlike those that the chaplain stated so baldly. Few state it that bluntly, but many clergy do feel that temptation, and some succumb to it.

One thing about this extreme of leadership—it is full of conflict and anger. And it usually generates more of both in the congregation. This approach tends to see history as the enemy, and all previous ideas of ministry as suspect, deserving only to be rooted out. I see the past of the congregation, on the other hand, as often flawed but as an enormous repository of experience, wisdom, and ministry that can become a ground upon which a new ministry can be built by clergy and laity.

At the other end of the scale the new pastor goes native—that is, "fits in," accepting all aspects of the congregation and community culture, so afraid of making a difference that he or she is concerned only not to rock any boats. In this case, the past is not eliminated; rather, the past rules over the future. The new pastor abdicates his or her special gifts for this place and simply becomes an inert piece of furniture that doesn't get in the way of congregational life continuing just as it has been in the past.

I see ministry as the heart of the congregation's life—a communal reality and a historical reality. It comes into being there in a particular group of people and in a particular context. It reflects the special gifts and weaknesses of a particular group of people and the story of their community of faith. It has been built in a dialogue in which many laity and a number of clergy have had roles and given their gifts. It is a building in which there have been all sorts of architects and carpenters, planners and painters, workers and dreamers, cooks and bottle washers.

And in my experience clergy have brought many differing gifts and differing resources to those congregations. Those gifts and resources are included in that history, even though those clergy may be long gone. The way we "do" congregation nowadays, it is the energy that comes from the live connection between laity and clergy that generates much life in the congregation and leads it to new places. When the clergy simply go native, they leave behind the special perspective and gifts they have for the community and its ministry, and much of the energy for new life evaporates. When clergy cease to bring any outside perspective and gifts to the congregation, they abdicate their ability to contribute to the life of the congregation.

The other side of this extreme is that it tends to be very, very peaceful. People may ignore this kind of ministry, but they probably will not fight it.

The first developmental task, coming to terms with the past, opts against these two extremes. It means taking the time to mine the successes and failures of the past and from them build a foundation for new maturity. Coming to terms with the past means the congregation comes to a place where it is able to look at its past, lay to rest its ghosts, value its heroes and heroines, honor its special story, forgive itself for its faults, and gain energy for a new stage of its journey.

I frequently think of my work as a pastor or as a consultant as that of "exorcising demons." Not in the way the movie *The Exorcist* exploited, but in the mundane work of helping people gain power over irrational fears and influences that past experience or people have over them. At times of pastoral change we often discover giants (some good ones and some bad ones) of clergy or lay leaders who cast a long shadow over the way things are done in the congregation. Just as there are great persons and great leaders who cast a long shadow, there are people who leave negative or hurtful marks in a congregation. Particularly when there has been misbehavior that leads to departure (a pastor who engages in sexual misbehavior; a clergy or lay leader who misappropriates funds; an employee who has to be fired; a pastor accused of plagiarism) the pain is often exacerbated by a cloak of secrecy—some people in the congregation are "in the know" and many others are "in the dark." Such memories leave a lot of pain behind.

Emotions we have about pastors are often highly charged. Pastors trigger feelings—good and bad—in those they work with in a congregation. Remembering experiences with past pastors is quite likely to touch levels of people's lives that are not touched by anyone other than a family member, parent, or sibling. Losing a pastor can be a hard emotional blow, triggering all the emotions of grief—it is not strictly a rational exercise. The emotions one associates with grief are likely to be present in the congregation that is losing its pastor—unreasonable anger, debilitating depression, simple denial, bargaining, and, with luck, acceptance flowing through congregation members—in different proportions and at different times. These are emotional responses to the loss of the pastor, not rational states that can be reasoned with or explained. People simply will get angry about ordinary glitches: a meeting that is not run well; an "ordinary" goof-up on an announcement list; an overlooked thank-you note. People will lose energy unexpectedly or even stop going to church in a sort of depression over the loss of the pastor. Others will simply ignore the whole thing, hoping it will either go away or get solved without disturbing anything. Others who loved the last pastor will vie to see if a new one exactly like the last one can somehow be chosen.

Contrariwise, those who did not like the last pastor will try to get an exact opposite person! Many of these are emotional responses, and it is the task of the congregation's leaders and search committee to allow time and discussion so these things can be worked through, not "answered." These emotional states will recycle themselves until the emotional gunpowder is used up. In time those emotions will move to the back burners as there is growing acceptance of the loss accompanied by growing anticipation of the next stage of history. (That's what we mean by "coming to terms with history"!)

Because this book deals with a change of pastoral leadership and the leaving of one pastor, the focus here is on the special dynamics of that pastoral role. But there are other important dimensions of history that need to be brought into the conversation.

There are the *things* of the congregation—its buildings, the special memorials, its location, and how the story of how the physical plant was assembled. Talking about these physical things can help us unpack our emotional baggage and get ready to move on.

There are the stories and even jokes that are part of the congregation—the things that are told every year at the annual meeting, such as the memories of great moments: an unexpected success, a surprising discovery, a long-lost member's return. Deaths and births. The day the organ blew the fuses. The day the janitor got into the sacramental wine. Again, this is a time for revisiting those memories and treasuring them.

There are the people everyone remembers—the special Sunday school teacher, the choir director (the one from heaven and also the one from hell), the reader who lost his teeth saying "Deuteronomy," the visiting preacher who got locked into the men's room. You'll have your own list; every parish does. Take time to bring those stories back. Relish them. Allow people to tell them over and over.

Telling these stories, laughing together, and sometimes being on the point of tears together—all of this helps your congregation come to terms with its history. And the point of it is to make your story your support for moving into the future. It is helping set your compass for the story ahead and keeping you from being locked into the past.

Your history can block your future, or it can give you a foundation for your future. You can stay focused on what you used to be and try to recreate it. ("Why don't we just keep doing it the way we did it when the former pastor first came?") Or you can use that history like a launching pad. ("We've always been able to make lemonade out of the lemons we've been handed—I bet the next stage of our congregation will be far better than what we've known in the past!")

That is your first developmental task: to live into your history so that you are freed to go ahead into the future without crippling handicaps, without always looking back over your shoulder.

Work on that developmental task will occur at each of the sequential steps—most obviously during termination and self-study, but there will be dimensions that come up all through the time between pastors. As a matter of fact, you are likely to find it so engaging that it will become a regular part of congregational life, reflected in dinners and retreats, meetings and festivals, even as you begin making new history with the new pastor. When you welcome your new pastor, you may want to gather around him or her and retell some of those same stories, thus bringing the new pastor into your story.

The Second Developmental Task: Discovering a New Identity

Congregations, like people, tend to get a fix on who they are at particular times, then stick with that identity until something comes along that shakes them out of their ruts. Many of us remember being startled at looking in a mirror and discovering white hair that has replaced the youthful black hair we remember. Our self-identity changes in fits and starts.

I remember a congregation that had a sense of itself as a congregation made up of young couples with lots of children. When I looked at the people in that congregation, they were all well into middle age and their children were mostly off at college or work. Many of them were grandparents. But in the heady years in which that congregation started, they *had* been young couples, and they did a lot of planning and programming around family life and Sunday school for young children.

The time when a pastor leaves is a rich time for a congregation to update its perception of itself. It is a time to learn what new kinds of people have become part of their life (I remember myself trying to do this once and being astonished to discover that the largest single demographic group in the parish was of single women heads of household). What has happened to the profile of ages in the congregation and of the kinds of work the people are engaged in? This is a time for counting things and comparing to old counts—who are the pledgers or regular contributors and where do they live? If you've got some people with an instinct for numbers, turn them loose on the records of marriages and baptisms—try to find out where those people are and what's happened to them. You may be surprised at how many people with significant links to the congregation feel neglected but are open to reconnecting.

What about the *parish*? I have been sloppy in using the words *parish* and *congregation* fairly interchangeably. In fact, the words have different connotations, coming from different histories of "church." *Congregation* tends to reflect the more evangelical traditions of the "free church" movements and is very widely used in American Protestantism. The experience of the local church in that tradition more characteristically thinks of the sum total of the people associated with that local institution. It is oriented to the people who make up the worshiping community.

Up until now, I have been talking about the self-identity of the *congregation*—the people who are about to lose their pastor. Now I want to switch gears to talk about that local church as it is experienced in other religious traditions—the churches who look back on a history of being "established" churches, related to the political world. In such contexts, the local church is called *parish*, which denotes an amount of territory, a place with geographic bounds. As *congregation* speaks of the people who go to the local church, *parish* speaks of the area surrounding that local church and all the inhabitants thereof. Those two meanings are often present when people talk about their local church, but they differ in that in the first case the emphasis is on the people who worship together; in the second, the emphasis is on the area with its total population.

The point here is that there really are *two* self-identifications that need to be rethought when the pastor leaves. I have been talking about the local church's identity as a congregation, but thought also needs to be given to the local church's identity as parish. This simply means getting a new fix on what is going on in the community in which this local church is geographically located. Just as the congregation needs to see how its membership has shifted and changed since it last formed its identity, even so the sense of identity of the community needs to be rethought.

This is a time to do demographic studies of the area around the church. How has the economy changed? What kinds of immigration has affected the area? What has happened to the age profile of the community? What has happened to the level of poverty, and what different ethnic groups are part of the area now? And, of course, how do those data fit with similar data from the membership of the congregation?

As the church works with these data, it is likely to have lots of surprises connecting its congregation with its sense of parish or "turf." The church I go to on Sundays is on the corner of Massachusetts and Wisconsin Avenues in Washington, D.C. As a congregation, we consist of some 1,500 people residing all over the Washington metropolitan area, many working in jobs related to the U.S. government or other professional jobs, with an increasing number of retired people. We are thin, but growing, in children and young people. As a parish, we sense a special call to minister to our northwest Washington neighborhood's many apartment dwellers, but we also feel a responsibility to be a presence of faith in many governmental agencies in which our people work, in many neighborhoods throughout the region, and we have a sense of ecumenical partnership in caring for the homeless and hungry who live in the area. All of those are part of our self-identity, but all are also changing every year.

Most denominational offices can put congregations in touch with agencies that can provide elaborate demographic studies. This is a time to indulge in such study—but with a warning: many demographic studies are absolutely inaccessible to intelligent human beings without someone who can lead you through the lists of data and different colored maps. Many cities and counties have planning agencies that will be delighted to help you learn what you need to know about the context in which this local church exists and help you get a new sense of identity. What's good is that people of those agencies are paid to bring such presentations to local groups—and many are good at it.

Churches, of course, will find it important to their own identity to study the similarities and differences between their congregation and their parish. In examining that tension they are likely to get new insight into what God may be calling the church to pay attention to.

At the time of pastoral search, this rediscovery of identity is an important ingredient in thinking about what you need leadership in facing. All through the seven sequential steps you will have time to touch this sense of your emerging identity, but it will be particularly true as you do your self-study and translate that self-study into the profile of the kind of leadership you think you need.

The Third Developmental Task: Allowing for Needed Leadership Changes

While a church is going through a pastoral change, there is one particularly important dynamic that leaders need to note and help to happen. Pastors tend to draw close to them a group of leaders who, over time, come to enjoy contributing time and energy to help lead the work of the congregation. Often these leaders come to leadership because they enjoy the pastor's way of doing things and enjoy working with him or her.

It is absolutely natural and healthy for some of those who have been long-time dependable leaders to see the change of pastors as a time to step back from the same degree of day-to-day involvement. It is also just as natural for some of the members of the congregation to see the leaving of one pastor and the coming of another as a good time to begin offering their own different gifts of leadership.

It is the work of the leaders of the congregation and the search committee to look for opportunities to facilitate this healthy movement of members into new leadership positions and allow those who want to step back from leadership to do so. The search committee itself is an opportunity for using at least a few people who have not been leaders before but have obvious leadership gifts. And on the fringes of the search committee there are other places where new leadership can be recruited: you will need leaders to help with the events surrounding the leaving of the previous pastor; you will need special groups to work with demographic data and even, perhaps, to administer questionnaires or manage group meetings. You will need many leaders and volunteers to manage the events in which the new pastor is welcomed and introduced to the community as well as to the congregation itself.

I still remember visiting a church when I was asked to preach soon after the pastor had left. After the worship service a member of the congregation came up to me at coffee hour, apparently impressed by my sermon. (I'll be honest—this doesn't always happen, which may be why I remember it!) She said to me, "You know, I am on the search committee, and I wonder if I could have your permission to put your name on our list." Somewhat flattered, I replied, "I really feel called to what I am doing, but tell me what your role on the committee is." "I've only been here seven years," she said, "so I've been named the newcomer on the committee." I don't believe she knew how much she had just told me about the congregation. Seven years and still being treated as a newcomer! That congregation had a different definition of "new" from the one I had. But at least I saw evidence that someone in the congregation was trying to open space for new leadership to be brought in.

All the leaders of the congregation need to have open eyes during this whole process of changing pastors. More and more laypeople will need to be called on for ideas and help, and leaders need to locate that potential and move those persons into roles for the future. It is also important to allow people who have led long and well to back away from leadership. They will be needed again, but many of them need a sabbatical from direct responsibility for a time. Continuing leaders need to use this time especially to find their replacements from those who are ready to step forward.

The Fourth Developmental Task:
Rediscovering the Denomination

For many congregations, the relationship with the denomination is filtered through the lens of the current pastor. If the pastor is deeply involved in denominational issues, the congregation is likely to hear much about those issues. If he or she is not so involved, the congregation may begin to be distanced from what is going on in the denomination (in this I mean both the regional form of the denomination and the national/international structures). It is almost irrelevant whether the denomination is "connectional" or "nonconnectional" in its polity.

Those two terms point to a continuum of relationship that ranges from a close, interactive relationship to a distant, independent relationship with denominational entities. I have found that the specific denomination is not as important in this continuum as is the relationship—in some denominations that have a high value for congregational independence and autonomy, many congregations have a very close relationship to what the regional church body is up to. At the same time, in denominations defined as closely linked, many congregations act as if they are totally separate from the regional body.

Those sets of relationship become habitual and reflect local and regional history, the personalities of many leaders over time, and the vision of the local pastor and congregational leaders. At the time of pastoral change, however, the local congregation is thrown into contact with the denomination in an active, direct way. I see this as a real asset and opportunity. Instead of being ruled by experience of previous generations and pastors, the congregation's leaders have an opportunity to explore what kinds of relationships they want the congregation to have with the denomination, especially if those relationships have not been strong. If there has been a close relationship, this is an opportunity to build linkages that better reflect how the congregation wants to build future links, which may be more independent.

I have found most regional and national denominational offices to have access to resources, ideas, and savvy people who can usually be helpful to congregations. They have training programs for leaders, resources (in media and print), and they know where other resources can be found. Sometimes they have contracts with companies that provide all kinds of other resources, demographic, consultative, and so forth.

Denominational offices also have access to professional dossiers of clergy and can help the congregation get them. They have a stake in the growth and health of each congregation as well. Generally, they are in the business of helping congregations.

The time of pastoral change is an opportunity for the congregation to get a first-hand experience of how the denomination works, how helpful its resources are, and how sensitive it is to the congregation's real situation. Because you *have* to work with them at such a time (they often are one of the places that is best at helping you locate names—of interim pastors, of consultants, of potential pastor candidates), this is a good time to make the connections that you think will be helpful when the new pastor comes and into the future.

Don't forget that in the future you will, from time to time, need some help. Denominational groups can provide support and training for ordained leaders, programs the congregation cannot mount on its own, help when conflict hits or when stress is overwhelming. It often can help with financial advice. Also, when denominations are doing their work well, they can challenge the congregation to greater effectiveness.

The point? During the change of pastors there will be a number of opportunities to check what resources the denomination can provide and an opportunity to bring them into a more effective collegial linkage with you and thus be more effective in doing what you need to do together.

The Fifth Developmental Task: Commitment to New Directions in Ministry

If you just stick with it on the journey through the inevitable seven steps outlined in chapter 3, you will end up with a new pastor. The way our systems are set up, it is almost impossible to end up without a pastor. That's not the real question, however.

The question is, is that all you want? Is all you want a hired hand to manage the preaching and the worship and to make out the annual reports to the denomination?

The whole point of this book is to help you to go through the things you have to do in such a way that you come out in a new place. I want you to come out with new visions of what God wants you to be and do. I want you to come out with some real new commitments about what is important and what is not. I want you to know yourself to be in a team with others equally committed to a new future and a new ministry.

The other side? Yes, I want you to know that the pastor you have selected has also selected you and that you are bound to each other for a purpose: to build a worshiping, working community of faithful people who have discovered a direction of ministry and intend to pursue it. Together.

I make no demand that you do all this the "right" way, because I do not know what that way is for you. I expect you will make mistakes and miss lots of opportunities on your journey of the next months or years. Some things you will have to invent as you go along. Some things that go wrong you will have to figure out how to fix.

But all along, from the moment you discover your pastor is leaving until well after the new pastor is in place, you are journeying toward that common commitment to new life and new mission. You are not in a "hiring process." You are in a transformation process. You will be transformed and your new pastor will be transformed.

This business of finding new commitment to a new ministry is not what you do at the end of the process, it is how you approach every step of the way. It is behind how you deal with each other and your former pastor as you grieve and celebrate your losses and accomplishments. It is part of your discovering how to do what you have to do. It is at the heart of your studying your past and your future needs and looking at your community's needs. It is in how you make your decisions, and it is the basis for your negotiations with your new pastor.

5

Important Fellow Travelers

Every time I get a panicky call as I did from Al about having lost a pastor, one of the things I try to do is put that person in touch with some of the many resource people who can help. In this chapter I want to tell you about some of the resource people you may need to access over the next months.

All church bodies try to be sure that congregations like Al's and yours have a variety of resources and resource people for when the change-of-pastor time comes. For several months or even a year or two, you will need these resources on a regular basis; then, when you no longer need them, they'll be put in storage, as it were, until the next time you need help. In the meantime these resources will be assisting other congregations and being continuously updated to provide the best help possible.

I want to describe five of the actors from the church system that you may use, or at least meet, in the next few months. If I knew where you were, I could probably give you a telephone number or two. The resource people are these:

1. Your bishop or executive
2. Search (or Interim) consultants
3. Interim pastors

4. Board members (or vestry, council, or session members, depending on the denomination)
5. Search committee members

The first three of these are outside your congregation, but the last two are *in* your congregation. I deal with those two here because in a real way their operation during the time between pastors is a new part of their life for which they may need new training or orientation. You may need to bring in outside resources to help with their training. Keeping clear about the different functions these persons have will make you a better participant in the process.

The First Leadership Role: The Bishop or Executive

The bishop or executive probably has many relationships with the congregation already. Some members of the congregation will be well acquainted with him or her because of previous encounters, perhaps in a task force or commission of the judicatory. That is one of the problems, however: members of your congregation may harbor grudges or unreal hopes of the executive's office based on bad or good relationships they've had with this bishop *or his or her predecessor!* Here is a chance for a fresh start—work to open communication up so you can discover what the current policies and resources are and how to work with this part of your church system. There is no better time to try to clear away any past misunderstandings as you get started in this new relationship.

The bishop or executive is the point person for the denomination at the time of a pastor's leaving. That is, he or she is the one with access to the denomination's protocols and rules about what is to be done and by whom. He or she knows what kinds of resources or staff are available. One of the first telephone calls you need to make after the pastor announces a resignation is to arrange a meeting with the executive or bishop. The pastor sometimes has already told this person about the resignation, but lay leaders need immediately to get into the conversation. And they need to be connected directly, not through the pastor; again, this is an opportunity to open up the kind of direct communication you will need through the period until a new pastor is in place. If somebody at the church does not phone the executive or bishop, this is no time for reticence—the bishop or executive needs to take the initiative and get in touch to set up meetings and conversations.

I think it is critical to have the executive or bishop personally on site in the parish as soon as possible. He or she does not have to provide all the resources that are needed during the interim, but the congregation's leaders will need reassurance from outside. Many of the resources can be delivered by a staffperson, but I do not want to underrate the importance of having the one the people recognize for regional leadership actually being present as the process begins. He or she needs to meet with the official church board, if possible before a search committee is appointed. I recommend that the retiring pastor be present to welcome the executive or bishop but that the pastor not stay for the whole meeting.

Larger executive offices will have a staffperson who has full-time responsibility for helping congregations with the pastoral change process. In smaller judicatories that staffperson may be part-time. In this description of what needs to be done, some things should be done early by the bishop or executive, but other things can be done equally well by the staffperson days or weeks later.

The main function of the bishop or executive at this point is pastoral care of the congregation. A secondary issue is the pastoral care of the retiring pastor. Most congregations at the time of the resignation of a pastor are thrown into a mixture of confusion, anxiety, grief, and panic. Leaders feel the panic and have to deal with phone calls from members sharing all the other feelings. Let it also be said, there will be members of the congregation also who feel delight and pleasure at the leaving of the pastor. That does not make the change coming up any easier. At times it is much more difficult to deal with the pastor's antagonists than his or her supporters.

Whatever the mix of emotions, the moment of the pastor's resignation leaves congregational leaders feeling a strong need for clarity, for direction, and for support in their leadership. The bishop or executive needs to take that seriously and address it directly in those early meetings with congregational leaders.

Here are some of the things the executive or bishop needs to deal with early on:

1. Reassurance that there *is* a map of where they are and what they are going to need to do in finding a new pastor
2. Reassurance that the judicatory will help them maintain the worship and pastoral life of the congregation
3. The name of someone they can call at church headquarters to get information or answers to questions that may come up
4. Orientation to policies or recommendations (being sure to distinguish which is which) on a number of things they may need to know, such as:
   a. Search committee membership and method of appointment/election
   b. Usual policies about relationship to former pastors
   c. What the denominational or regional practices/ policies are about involvement with nominations to the pastorate

d. Information about access to consultative assistance and how to get it
e. Information about availability of interim pastors and the process of getting one
f. Information about access to various lists of books, consulting and planning agencies, etc.
g. Information about how to access those who can do background checks on nominees
h. At the appropriate time, access to samples of clergy contracts/covenants/agreements such as are used by others

This is not an exhaustive list. There will be other things the congregation will want from its bishop or executive's office. In our experience the door is usually open from both ends for further inquiries. The point is that both parties—the office and the congregation—must keep that door open and use it whenever a need arises.

Farther along in the work of the search, the executive or bishop needs to try to communicate something of substance in addition to what is on the list above. Here are several of the important inputs the congregation needs from the church outside itself. Denominational polity may structure this through the bishop or executive, but where that structure does not explicitly provide it, the congregation ought to find a way to get it:

1. What is the "story" of the congregation as seen by outsiders?
2. What do outsiders (in the community, in the church or denomination at large) expect or need this congregation to be in terms of its mission? What do others see the church called to be?
3. What have been this congregation's characteristic strengths and weaknesses?

The outside voice needs to push the congregation and its search committee to be clear and direct, not to generalize but to be specific. All of this information needs to help shape the profile.

I have described more than probably can be done. It is also true that congregations sometimes do not want to hear what is said to them. My point is not that it be accepted, but that the bishop or executive try to see that the messages are sent with clarity. The congregation has the right to determine which messages fit and which do not.

The executive or bishop has a full plate already, even before this congregation's pastor resigned. The "other" stuff will press for attention. I want to say this very directly, however, to any bishop or executive who is reading: *there is no one place where your leadership and ministry can have more payoff for your congregations, for your pastors, or for your denomination than in the dynamics of the changing of pastors.*

Over a single decade, an executive or bishop who focuses primary attention to this dynamic will have a hand in shaping almost every congregation in her or his judicatory. There is no other one place that has that kind of in-depth payoff.

The Second Leadership Role: The Interim Consultant

The word *consultant* is packed with many meanings. In churches there are three primary uses for the word.

First, a consultant is somebody with special knowledge that you hire because you need that knowledge. There are consultants in organizational structure who will help you develop your own organizational structure from the many types with which the consultant is familiar. A pension and benefits consultant will bring a vast knowledge of taxes and benefit plans and will help you design a system that fits your organization. An architectural consultant knows buildings and building materials and can help you put together a building that fits your needs. In this section I'm not talking about this kind of consultant.

Second, a consultant is somebody who has wisdom or insights of various kinds and is willing to be your advisor. You trust them and hire them and they either help you or don't. I'm not talking about this kind of consultant.

A third kind of consultant is someone who is a specialist in how individuals and groups work together to get the things done that they want to accomplish, meanwhile strengthening the group and the individuals in their ability to accomplish other things. Some call this a "process consultant." That is the closest of these three to a description of an "interim consultant."

The primary work of the interim consultant is to help the people appointed to the search committee to become an effective work team that helps manage the procedures (the sequential steps) of a pastoral search so that the processes (the process steps) of development can occur in a congregation that is searching for a pastor.

To do that, the interim consultant needs to have a basic knowledge of the procedural steps and considerable training in the processes of development that I have outlined in this book.

Specific areas in which the consultant needs to be able to help the search committee are these:

1. How the individual members can become a team and learn to work together to develop a work plan
2. How to organize complex tasks and see that they are kept on track with the work plan
3. How to facilitate communication with the office of the bishop or executive

4. How to assure that the church board and the search committee develop trust in one another and are clear about their boundaries
5. How to train search committee members in a variety of tasks: gathering data, analyzing it, and producing a parish profile; doing interviews and keeping records of nominees and of their references; analyzing personnel records/dossiers from the denomination; designing job descriptions; making complex choices and decisions; designing intergroup communication and carrying it out; dealing with misunderstandings and conflicts
6. How to make and complete contracts
7. How to maintain liaison with the regional church office

It is essential that the consultant be responsible to, and therefore the employee of, the congregation, not the regional church office. It is sometimes necessary for the church office to assist the congregation in paying for the consultant, but it needs to be understood that the consultant is not hired to do what the judicatory wants but what the congregation wants. The congregation needs to maintain the ability to hire and fire this person, otherwise the consultant is acting as a staffperson for the judicatory.

Because these relationships are critical, I recommend that the judicatory put together a list of the people it trusts to carry out this role and make that list available to the congregation. If the congregation needs financial help in paying for the consultant, that is a matter for the congregation to negotiate with the judicatory. But it needs to be clear that the consultant is not "reporting" to the judicatory other than in those areas the congregation agrees to.

I still remember with fondness the report I got from one congregation that had used a consultant. When I asked what that person had done during the search, the reply came back,

"Well, I don't exactly remember. I'm not sure exactly what she did. Certainly nothing we couldn't have done without her. But then," the reply continued, "we weren't doing it before she came, and I don't think we'd have done it half as good if she hadn't made us."

That's not a bad description of what must have been a pretty good consulting relationship.

I recommend that every congregation going through a pastoral change use the best consultative help they can get. There is no better way to help the congregation's leaders work effectively to get the pastoral change accomplished on time.

The Third Leadership Role:
The Interim Pastor

The interim pastor is a full-time (or part-time) pastor who takes on the full pastoral leadership of a congregation for the period between installed pastors.

There are many reasons for using such a skilled person, the most important being that the leadership of a congregation often finds itself overloaded with responsibility during the period between installed pastors. The management of the search process is a significant call for leadership energy, and the board can find itself overwhelmed by trying also to locate a regular preaching and worship leadership, handle the regular and crisis pastoral care, and continue all the community building pastors provide in congregations. Having a professional on call to cover those bases can relieve leadership for the tasks of the transition.

I do not think all congregations necessarily need a fully trained interim pastor—that is a judgment call for the bishop or executive and the leadership of the parish board. In some cases all that is needed is someone to come in to cover the worship. There are, however, several situations in which I have come to believe the special skills of a highly trained interim pastor are required:

1. *An interim pastor is needed if the previous pastorate was a very long one.* I think of "long" as 12 years or more, but that is not a highly defined term! The point is that there are special problems that occur when a pastor has been around a long time—for instance, the grief issues are often more complex. Sometimes negative feelings are triggered by the fact that any new pastor leads the worship services at a different "pace," requiring people to adjust to sudden small surprises every week. In the long run, such change needs to happen before a "permanent" pastor comes in. The interim pastor gives the people a chance to adjust to new leadership in little things but also in larger ones. There are also practical things nobody seems to think about: the departing pastor knows where all the keys and the light switches are! He or she knows what all the little memorial funds are for and what bank they are in. One of the mundane tasks of the interim pastor is to clear up the clutter and sort out things that need sorting out.

2. *An interim pastor is needed if the previous pastorate ended in unhappy conflict and polarization.* I have mentioned before the situation of pastorates ending after pastoral misbehavior, where the need for such help is self-evident. Here I am talking about the kind of conflict within the congregation, whether it led to a "firing" or not, that results in angry groups confronting one another, with some coming out "winners" and others "losers." In such a case it is imperative to get an interim pastor who has special skills in conflict management and who can help clean up the mess before another pastor comes in for a longer term. Conflicted congregations are much more likely to continue the conflict into the next pastorate than they are to "solve" the conflict. The next pastor is more likely to become a victim of the underground conflict than to be able to overcome it. The change of pastorates is a terribly

important time to address such deep-seated wounds. Often judicatory pressure or influence needs to be exerted at such a time; people in the conflict have unreasonable hopes that "it will all get better" or that "it's unhealthy to dwell on all that unpleasantness." My experience tells me that you'd better get somebody on board who can help deal with it, or the next pastor has a good chance of being crucified on the conflict that's already there.

3. *An interim pastor is also needed when the congregation is a large, multistaffed entity.* The interim selected for such a situation needs to have management skills and staff supervisory skills adequate for the large congregation. The congregation's board usually cannot handle all the management of such a church, but the need for management can overwhelm them. A usually unhappy decision is to "appoint" or "promote" one of current staffpersons to be head of staff. I say this is usually unhappy because it often triggers resentments in other staffpersons when you need the team to continue working together. It also often leads to parties in the congregation lobbying for that person to become the "senior" pastor. In the long run it also complicates the life of the next pastor, who might want to keep that staffperson but has to "demote" her or him to do so. Having an experienced interim pastor helps the transition but also helps avoid some problems.

A trained interim pastor can help the congregation in a number of ways that may be difficult for anyone else to do:

a. *Intervene with the retiring/leaving pastor.* Sometimes, with the best intentions, the pastor who is leaving meddles and interferes with what the congregation's leadership must do or with tasks like the pastoral care. An interim pastor can be very direct in a way that laypeople in the congregation may not feel comfortable being. He or she can "enforce" agreements that have already been made defining boundaries, or, if people forgot to establish boundaries, the interim can insist that they be defined (like when the former pastor may come back for funerals or marriages or baptisms; what is appropriate and what is inappropriate in regards to the former pastor attending church worship services after leaving its pastorate; when the former pastor should vacate the office and/or the pastoral residence; what happens to the pastor's discretionary fund). Few board chairs feel comfortable dealing with the former pastor about these things.

b. *Rattle cages that need rattling.* There are always things that are operating poorly or inefficiently. The interim pastor comes in with a mandate to clean such things up. Who cleans the worship vestments and who takes care of the choir rehearsal room? How are the janitorial services being supervised? Who makes the decisions about who leads prayers or readings and who trains them so it is well done?

c. *Check the financial situation.* Interim pastors need to be sharp inquisitors about what is happening in the finances of the congregation, looking for neglected areas. Congregations often have very able financial people, but pastors are often not good supervisors or leaders in financial matters. The interim pastor does not come in as an auditor, but he or she needs to look at the overall picture and bring to the board the needs that surface. There is often a need to take a "look-see" at the adequacy of the oversight mechanisms for reserve funds or special memorial funds.

d. *Blow the whistle on irresponsible giving.* The interim pastor is probably freer than any other pastor to call the congregation to attention if it has gotten lackadaisical about the level of its giving and stewardship. This is a particular way that an interim, working with the congregation's board, can make an enormous difference in the pastorate of the next pastor.

e. *Help the board know how to work with the denomination and with its consultative help.* Trained interims understand their role is neither to be the messenger for the denomination nor to do the work of a consultant, but to be a mediator of both sets of relationships. Good interims improve the efficacy of a good consultant.

f. *Teach the congregation how to manage relationships and end them well.* Interim pastors work within a contractual framework and help the congregation learn about boundaries and how to keep them clear. The trained interim also knows from the beginning that he or she is never to become a candidate for the permanent position. This really can help the congregation in making its decisions and also in moving beyond the previous pastor. The interim pastor also gets a chance to model a good departure!

The Fourth Leadership Role: Lay Board Member

Board members in every denomination have books of order or board handbooks or sets of canons, often written in ecclesiastical gobbledygook, outlining the responsibilities and tasks of the office. In each place those rules are adapted to local conditions, and are usually brought out of the closet only when something goes wrong. In this brief section I want simply to point to areas in which I think the tensions and dynamics of going through a pastoral change may modify or shift those tasks.

When a pastor resigns, the first thing for the board to do is to get its executive or bishop (or the assigned staffperson) in. They will know the relevant sections of the rules and they will have considerable experience in working with other boards and answering the kinds of questions board members have. They can give you a quick orientation to what you will need to do. Get clear early on what authority the board has: Does it make the decision about the next pastor? Does someone have a veto power? Does the congregation put the matter to a congregational vote?

Ask the bishop, executive, or staffperson how they can help you: Can they give you lists of supply clergy for Sunday services? Do they have policies about the use and payment for such persons? Do they have access to lists of interim pastors? Access to interim consultants? Suggestions for self-study or mission study for the congregation? What do they recommend for the make-up of a search (or pastor-seeking) committee? What about the budget for such a committee? Ask them about anything that confuses you, and also ask how you can continue to use them.

Over several weeks, as a lay board member, here are some of the things you'll need to be thinking about and acting on:

1. *The use of an interim pastor and interim consultant.* If you decide to use an interim pastor, you will need a process for interviewing that person. If you want to use the interim consultant, you need to coordinate with the search committee; they should choose the consultant.
2. *A job description for the search committee.* This should include information such as how many people, what general timeframe, what kind of staff or budget they may count on, the extent of the search (national or regional), whether you want them to bring in one name or several, who on the board will be the liaison for information, and so forth.

3. *Who is to be on the search committee.* Here are some suggestions: between 6 and 12 persons, but certainly no more than 15 or 16 who will commit the time and energy for 18 months to two years; people who are respected members of the congregation; people who represent different points of view, but not people who are so rigid they cannot compromise; people who can work with others; people who are not all devotees or opponents of previous pastor; and people with particular ideas and skills.

4. *Communications.* Clarify who is in charge of releasing information to the congregation and to the public. Clarify how and when the search committee will report to the board and to the congregation.

5. *Negotiating power.* As the search proceeds, be sure to have in place an understanding between the board and the search committee about who negotiates what with the candidates and what parameters the search committee has in describing the work, its pay, benefits, and housing even before "negotiations" begin.

6. *Shared concerns.* Arrange a way for the concerns of the board or the search committee to be shared with each other and negotiated if need be.

7. *Congregational support.* Maintain strong support of the work of the congregation. Be at church every Sunday. Step in to help wherever needed.

The Fifth Leadership Role:
Search Committee Member

The role of search committee member is one of the toughest and most rewarding positions one can have in a local congregation. It is tough for many reasons, but especially because it often comes at awkward times in light of one's other commitments, and it is very demanding of time. It is rewarding in that search committee members often tell us the experience was a highlight of their lives: building strong new relationships within the congregation, meeting church leaders in many parts of the country, being challenged to rediscover what "church" means to one personally, and to have a real hand in shaping the future of one part of the church.

There probably is no lay role in the church with such a long-range potential for ensuring the future of the congregation. The search committee is involved in no less than trying to discern what God is calling the congregation to be and who God is calling to be its professional leader.

Over the course of the search, committee members will experience the breadth of the church, the variety of its leaders, the way churches in other places are responding to the changing place of the church in society.

If you are a committee member, you will also be involved in trying to discover both the congregation's strengths and its areas of weakness. You will discover challenges to which you will be called to respond. You will meet a number of splendid clergy, and you will probably find some you'd just as soon not have met. You'll see the whole ball of wax.

You will have to learn some hard give-and-take with the other members of the committee—how to honestly, even violently, disagree yet still work together and find ways to compromise. You will discover confidential information that you have to take to your grave with you and never let on that you've heard it at all.

In the course of the search, after you work on a parish self-study, you will have to deal with a list of potential candidates, sometimes a list longer than your arm. You'll have to learn to differentiate among them, learning more and more about them. You'll very likely discover some "favorites" on the list and get partially committed to one or more of them. Then you'll have the hard job of working with the other committee members to choose the one you think God wants more than the ones any of you is pushing.

It isn't easy, and nobody can tell you from the front end exactly what you'll discover. But this work is for real, for keeps—and what you and the committee come up with will make a long-term difference in your parish. Not only that, but the *way* you do the job will help the congregation move beyond its past and start toward new visions.

What could be more satisfying?

But. But. Accepting a role on the search committee commits you for a very significant amount of time. For a year, a year and a half, or sometimes even more you will be involved in intense meetings (many times weekly meetings of two to three hours each). As the search comes toward its end, you may well have to commit five to seven weekends for visiting congregations to meet pastors on their home ground.

It's a big task, but it's an important one. Of course it's not easy. But the Lord never promised us it would be easy.

6

Changing Pastors
and Change Itself

Why is it so hard to change a congregation?

I get asked that question a lot. My work almost always has to do with congregations in one way or another. I help clergy with things they want to accomplish. I work with church boards who want to strengthen their life or install some kind of plan or program. I work with people who are angry with what's going on in their congregation, and I work with people who are depressed with what's happening (or *not* happening) in their congregation. I work with groups and people who are enthusiastic about where they are going and with others who are afraid of what's happening in their congregations.

What's the bottom line? It's simple: there are a lot of people who care very deeply about their congregation. Their congregations mean a lot to them. Almost all of them have a gut feeling that things could be better than they are.

Many, many of them have experienced frustration, having tried every way they know to make things better and found that no matter how hard they try things don't change. Or they change so slowly, they've given up.

There is good news and bad news in all this. The good news is that when change *does* come, it is possible that it will stay around a long time. Another way of saying that is that congregations have a wealth of stability in them. They resist change. They are organizations in homeostasis, in equilibrium—they tend to stay put. They are like a sailboat with a deep and heavy keel that won't flip over or turn around on a dime. That's not a bad thing.

The bad news is that congregations are heavily resistant to the very efforts people put into them to make them better—or at least better as those people define "better." Congregations, seen in another nautical analogy, are like steadily moving, heavily loaded barges that tend to go relentlessly in one direction either until they hit something that sinks them or until they are grappled by a powerful tugboat that can wrestle them onto another course.

Many human institutions share those characteristics. The literature of management is full of the dilemmas about how one can take recalcitrant companies or committees or organizations and get them to change. What Al Shepherdson's congregation and your congregation is facing is that basic problem of human community—dealing with organizational change—the fascination some people have for it, the allergic reaction others have to it, and the absolute necessity to find some way to hold those different groups in community while making necessary adjustments to the changing circumstances they share.

What I am talking about in this book is precisely this same issue: How do you change a human enterprise that's stuck in a way that doesn't destroy the people in it, that doesn't subvert its values, but that helps it adapt to the changing world around it? How do you do that in a way that affirms the people, affirms their basic values, and strengthens their effectiveness?

People in congregations and churches have struggled with that issue for millennia. In some sense this issue caused a split in the Eastern and Western churches in 1054 C.E. It lay behind Martin Luther's battle with Catholicism and the whole Protestant Reformation. Today it is part of the civil war between the evangelical and mainline church families, the conservative fundamentalist war with the liberal revisionists, and the challenge of Pentecostalism to non-Pentecostal churches.

How and on what basis do you move a resistant body in homeostasis through necessary adaptations to live constructively in a changed world? I don't have the answer. I do have a very strong clue, though, and I have a strategy.

A Clue and a Strategy about Change

The clue comes from comments by one of those wise old gurus—a behavioral scientist of the 1930s and '40s, Kurt Lewin.

Lewin made the point that the problem with human institutions is their very homeostasis. He noted that organizations are always stable because they are a balance of opposing forces held together, frozen in equilibrium, and they cannot change until that equilibrium is somehow broken. He stated a very simple prescription of three steps that had to be taken if one wanted to see change happen:

1. The frozen equilibrium had to be unfrozen.
2. The desired change had to be installed.
3. The organism/organization then had to be refrozen with the change in place.

Thousands of change efforts in churches have been stymied by the same thing that frustrates those who want to change other institutions. Every attempted strategy bangs head-on into something just as hard as an iceberg. Occasionally a small bit chips off, but the entity does not really change.

In the late 1960s many people across many denominations were working at how to change congregations. Many of us were "alumni" of movements that challenged the ordinary structures of the churches—the liturgical movement, the civil rights movement, the industrial mission movement, the early renewalist movements, the group dynamics movement. Everywhere we turned in the churches and in the communities we found ourselves blocked by icebergs resistant to change.

Within the Episcopal Church, a small group of us in an experimental program called Project Test Pattern, challenged both by the work of the Billy Graham Association and the World Council of Churches's emphasis on "The Missionary Structure of the Congregation," tried to adapt organizational change strategies for work with individual congregations.

Our work ran into the same frustration. Change did not come easily, even when the people in the congregation were given help to design and implement the changes they said they wanted. We did not know how, in Lewin's words, to "unfreeze" the system.

In January 1972, a group of us gathered to see if we could break the impasse. One person pointed us in a new, more modest direction. "If we don't know how to unfreeze it," he suggested, "why don't we see if we can locate when it gets unfrozen by itself?" Then he answered his own question, "Every congregation gets unfrozen when its pastor leaves." It was so obvious that it led Project Test Pattern into the first research into the pastor-changing process and to several publications. Much of what you find in this book began to be understood during that research and in the three decades of work and research that followed.

We learned that Lewin was indeed right. We had discovered a laboratory in which to implement institutional approaches to change that had long-range implications.

When pastors leave is indeed a moment of "unfreezing." It is a moment during which many of the forces holding the congregation immovable are loosened and opened up. It is a time at which the status quo can be questioned and explored without a sense of violation.

When the pastor leaves a congregation, everybody knows instinctively that the old cannot be replicated in the same old way anymore—that some things will have to be faced and some done differently in the future. It does not determine *what* should be changed or *how* it should be changed; it merely asserts that the status quo is "in play." This is a time in which some things *can* change, if we choose to make it happen, as opposed to other times when things *might* happen, but generally do not.

In Lewin's theory, this is the first step. When the pastor moves, the system is unfrozen. Change becomes possible.

In all our previous work with congregations, we had found that almost all efforts to assist change got used up in trying to loosen the system up. Committees, pastors, and planning commissions ground to a halt because resistance to any change was so pervasive in the system's equilibrium. Change agents broke down from butting their heads against the iceberg.

Our subsequent work was to try to identify what could be done to help the congregation take charge of and make decisions about what *kind* of new life they sought. We analyzed what happened sequentially as decisions were made about what direction to choose (see chapter 3) and what processes needed to happen for the new elements of life to be absorbed into the DNA of the congregation (see chapter 4).

That was following Lewin's second statement: defining and installing what was to be part of the new life.

Lewin's final admonition we came to see as what we called "start-up." That was an effort to rebuild a new equilibrium in which a new relationship was established where choices of the future became the agenda of a dialogue between the clergy and laity of the congregation.

That is where, for us, a direction turned into a strategy. The direction is to help your congregation and others move through this moment and take advantage of it. Your having lost a pastor is not a disaster at all; it is a moment fraught with possibility.

The strategy is to recognize that church renewal is an extraordinary gift from God. It comes where it will and when it will if we open ourselves to it. There are many ways it can be approached, and I value most of them—spiritual development, deeper theological engagement and education, prayer and retreat, more effective ministries of teaching and preaching, liturgical growth, ministry to the homeless and hungry. Renewal is born in many of those places.

But the one place I am certain that renewal touches the hundreds of congregations I know and have worked with is at the moment of a change of pastors. Therefore, I urge pastors and judicatories, laypersons and administrators to focus on that moment and encourage congregations to go as deep as they can when it happens. That does not denigrate any of the other ways in which congregations and Christians grow, but it is one place I know they *do* grow. More than that, it is a place that is a continuing resource. Years ago, Al's congregation lost a pastor. They've done well, but now they've lost another. The same will be true for you. Another moment will—or already has—come in which new life may occur.

What's more, the same opportunity will occur again in a few years. And again, and again. I tell the church to keep an eye on that point. Over time you will have many times of such potential for growth.

Conclusion

Al Shepherdson's congregation, years ago, lost a pastor. In that "unfrozen" moment they worked to choose a future and, surprisingly, did something they'd never done before—they chose a woman pastor. (That's all I *know* they did differently, but I suspect, from the way Al regards her and has worked with her, that she also brought a kind of collaborative leadership they had not experienced before.) That earlier period of unfrozenness led to "ingesting" a new kind of pastor and pastoral relationship, and that congregation is in a different place from the one I consulted with seven or eight years ago.

Let me make a radical point that will upset every clergyperson who reads this: that change of pastors in Al's congregation was probably a much bigger change event than anything Sarah Brookstone was able to accomplish as pastor, personally or professionally.

That is the truth for every pastor in every congregation, unless the pastor and the congregation can learn to work together so as to keep some of the "unfrozenness" in the way they work together after the new pastoral placement. The whole point of all the work during the interim and the startup is to try to keep that openness as part of the new DNA, whoever the new pastor may be.

The ministry Al Shepherdson lost was not Sarah Brookstone. The ministry that's been lost is the wonderful corporate life the congregation experienced—a life that had benefited from Sarah's real gifts, but a corporate ministry that had also pulled Al and many others into a leadership team, a ministry that seems to have broadened the educational program and that did a lot of other things I don't know about. Now, with Sarah Brookstone leaving, a new moment of unfreezing is ahead—a time in which lots of new things become possible.

That's what I'm telling you about your congregation. So you have lost or are about to lose your pastor. Honor what you have been and what he or she has meant. Celebrate that life.

Al Shepherdson was angry and in a panic when he told me his pastor was leaving. You probably have some of those feelings about what's happened to you.

I don't know if you've ever been told what happens when things end tragically. Sometimes it seems a little too simple. People say, "Whenever the Lord closes a door on you, He always opens another."

It may be simple, but it's true in this case. That congregation in Oklahoma City has come to the end of what turned out to be a fine pastorate. The ministry that was already there before that pastorate, before Sarah ever arrived to become their first woman pastor—that ministry is still there, stronger because she contributed to its strength. It's stronger because Al Shepherdson pitched in and became part of that ministry and now carries on within it.

The ministry of your congregation was already there before you got there and before your pastor got there. That ministry was a gift and a call from God. The leaving of your pastor opens the door to a new chapter and a new call. I have a lot of confidence in what God will do with you. And I hope this book gives you a helpful guide for the journey ahead of you.

Afterword

The bulk of this book has been heavily practical, offering the things one needs to think about and accomplish during the time between pastors. If that's all you need, you are through with this book. Put it aside until the new pastor submits her or his resignation—but remember that's likely to be in four to eight years! You'll pass this way again!

To be truthful, though, we who studied this "critical moment" found ourselves led further, and many who read this book will want to think about those other things—two major subjects in particular. The first is the continued story of how the trail of learning took us to *other* issues about strengthening the relationship between clergy and laity. I will try to identify resources you will find helpful in those areas. I call this "The Path of our Research." The second is to name some important general themes about change and churches that this research and study opened up for us. I call this "Strategic Hunches about Change in Congregations."

A. The Path of Our Research

In the years since 1974 when the Alban Institute picked up the learnings of the Episcopal experimental "Project Test Pattern," we kept our eye on actual congregations. We operated on the assumption that those congregations were where we would discover what was needed to make for strong parish-pastor relationships. This made our work "inductive," starting with observable data, drawing hypotheses to test. This made our work different from the general denominational work with congregations, which tended to take off from strong models—from history, from theological positions, from ideological commitments, from program objectives—of what congregations "ought" to be. We tried to let the congregation speak for itself, rather than having a mental template to which we tried to get a congregation to conform. We never totally succeeded; nevertheless, our intent always was to start with the thing itself (the congregation, the people, the pastor in *that* place at *that* time and what they were trying to do). My own underlying theory was that I believed each congregation was being called by God to be something special and that the process of getting there depended upon their choices and decisions. I was clear that it was not my job to make them conform to my idea of what a good congregation was!

The late Urban T. Holmes and I described this model of working from actual life as "doing theology from the ground up." We began with congregations, not theories about congregations.

As we began the Alban Institute, one of our key advisors, Jack Harris, gave us our first direction. He asked, "What happens in the first year after a pastor arrives?" He went on, "I'll bet that within that first year things happen that make or break the long-term relationship. Within that first year the course is set—toward increasingly creative ministry of clergy and laity or toward inevitable dissolution." That wise question shaped much of our early study. Having begun studying what happened in the time between pastors, we began to branch out to what happened after the new pastor was installed.

Our research was of four types—(1) anecdotal (interviewing every pastor or lay leader we could lay hands on during the early part of a pastorate); (2) group interviews (with groups like United Methodist pastors just after they had been placed in a new assignment, where we discovered they could also reflect on earlier appointment changes); (3) focused research efforts with target groups (such as Army chaplains accustomed to changing pastoral assignments every three years); and (4) collecting the research of others on the same set of dynamics. Particularly useful was the research that had been done by John C. Fletcher as he was designing the experiment in theological education that he led in the Washington area—the Interfaith Metropolitan Theological Seminary, or INTERMET. John interviewed 125 lay leaders about the clergy who had influenced them, and the interviews turned up a common trajectory in the first few years of ministry.

As data accumulated, we began publishing a series of monographs about what we had come to call the "pastorate start-up." Alban senior consultant Roy Oswald was the key writer, and the continuing popularity and usefulness of the publications gives a lie to the only wisdom we had found earlier: "Every new pastor has a honeymoon—he or she can do anything in the first year with no trouble." We found that definitely not to be true. Indeed, a pastor who operated that way was likely to have cut off constructive relationships with the congregation long before the first year was out.

There were unexpected new pieces. For instance, Roy discovered the importance of the final months of a pastor *before* the pastor actually leaves. He put what he learned on that topic in another long-time Alban best-seller, *Running Through the Thistles*.

Don Smith, then executive of the Vocation Agency of the United Presbyterian Church, asked us to go the next step—

to study the *first* pastoral start-up, that is, when new pastors made the transition from seminary to the pastorate. His research had picked up the fact that newer clergy found that transition particularly traumatic. After we got over being embarrassed that we had not thought about it first, we got to work. With the help of a small grant from the Lilly Endowment, we did the first study of what we called "the boundary." By "boundary" we intended to convey how different were the cultures of the seminary and the congregation—and so we studied what happened when new clergy crossed that boundary into the congregational culture. We did this in ten seminaries.

All of this research was fed back, as well as we could, into the different denominations and seminary programs. By 2003–2004, a number of funding agencies and national denominations were beginning to mount special programs to help clergy make the transition from seminary to congregation.

Other dimensions of the transition of clergy became clear as we worked. In more cases that we liked to think about, congregations secured new pastors only to have the new relationship blow up almost immediately. As we studied what was going on, we found that sometimes during a previous pastorate unhealthy dynamics had built up, leaving heavy scar tissue that the new pastor would run into without knowing what was going on. Sometimes it was the consequence of a serious conflict, sometimes it was the aftermath of clergy misbehavior, sometimes it was the result of very positive feelings for a pastor who had been around for two or three decades, and sometimes it was simply that the previous parish staff had developed one or more candidates for the senior position—and polarized the congregation. When something like that happened, we found the congregation needed not just the kind of help described in this book—but some intensive therapy.

In 1975 we began developing what we came to call "interim pastors" to be the special cadre who could come in and give special, intensive help with the transition. We never thought that every congregation would need such a specialist, but we came to think that *anything* was better than putting a new pastor into a situation in which such negative dynamics were already present that he or she had no chance. By and large, the denominations have had very ambiguous relationships with interim pastors, partly because interim pastors tend to be a feisty bunch who don't fit the mold. To help them gain access to collegiality and support, we helped them establish the national Interim Pastor Network.

These studies of transitions led us to two other special issues in pastor-parish relations. We discovered the "long-tenured pastorate" as a special category of pastorates, and tried to discover what made for creative ministry over the long haul when it was also clear that many other long pastorates went dead midway through. We also discovered that some pastors and congregations made good use of sabbaticals as ways to refresh ministry.

B. General Themes from Our Research

Here I simply want to note and describe some of the larger issues we ran across in our work with congregations. These issues came to bear in the change of pastoral leadership, but they are larger than that. They have implications for churches and other organizations far beyond the placement of clergy.

1. The theories in our heads and the reality on the ground are frequently two different things. The tendency in church systems is to treat the theory as the dominant reality and to dismiss the importance of what the reality on the ground is. Our experience has been that the system is unlikely to respond to any theory, suggestion, direction, or hope if it does

not connect directly to what the people in the situation accept as their reality. I do not dismiss the theory—indeed, we use many in our work—but I make the point that people engaged in change need to see that what they are experiencing is taken seriously.

2. The moment of "transition" is a pregnant moment in organizations. In this book we have focused on the transition of pastoral leadership. But in other research we have looked at *other* transitions that are equally pregnant. I want to urge colleagues to *see* transition—not as an uncomfortable interruption—but as the signal that significant changes are likely to occur, and that careful work on the transition may make it significantly more creative. That holds for *every* transition. Someone resigns in high dudgeon. An older person reaches retirement. A new class is elected to the board of the congregation. A high school class graduates. A family celebrates the birth of a child. Somebody dies.

My point? When transitions happen, life changes. We can help some of those transitions have saving power rather than damning power.

3. The word *boundary* is a concept that is very useful. When people cross boundaries from one way of being to another they are in a first-class learning moment. They are eager to learn how to *be* in the new place. There are all sorts of boundaries—you cross a boundary when you decide to go to church for the first time in a long while; when you agree to let your name go up for election to something; when you leave for or return from college or seminary; when you take a new job or quit an old one.

My point? Look for people on boundaries and help them have access to learning.

4. The word *research* is intimidating. But I hope less so as I have used it in this book. Research is just committing oneself to watching what happens carefully, gathering impres-

sions and data, sharing them with others for reflection, drawing working hypotheses, and then going on to the next thing that presents itself, using one's previous learning to set the stage. This is not "laboratory research," which is the concept that I think intimidates us. It is what we have come to call "action research," and it is within the capability of anybody reading this book. Act thoughtfully, watch what happens carefully, reflect, and use what you have learned to guide further action.

My point? Your congregation's ministry is far less than you'd like it to be and far less than what God intends. But you are not a victim—you can take power to act and to make that ministry stronger and more creative. Your new pastor, whoever he or she may turn out to be, will need colleagues like you to make it happen.

Notes

Chapter Two

1. John shared his research in one of the first monographs the Alban Institute published, *Religious Authenticity in the Clergy* (Washington, D.C.: Alban Institute, 1975). John went on to become a celebrated and widely published specialist in bioethical research. His untimely and tragic death in 2004 left us poorer in the worlds of religion and biology.

2. There's a lot of talk in churches about how to attend to the "wellness" or "health" of the clergy. I don't fight those initiatives, but I can't help thinking they are off-base for two reasons. First, it is condescending to clergy and infantilizes them. Second, I don't think you get healthy clergy by holding their hands (sorry, I think *I'm* being unfair here!); you get healthy clergy by seeing to it that they are strong, effective leaders working with strong, effective laity. The answer is in helping them do a good job, not taking care of them.

Chapter Three

1. This monograph, no longer in print, was first published in 1974 by Project Test Pattern, an experimental program of the Episcopal Church. Its author was the Reverend Dr. William A. Yon of Chelsea, Alabama.

2. See *Running Through the Thistles* by Roy M. Oswald (Washington, D.C.: Alban Institute, 1978). This is one of the few resources for pastors and congregations trying to make this way through these weeks before the pastor leaves.

3. See *Restoring the Soul of a Church*, edited by Nancy Myer Hopkins
   and Mark Lanser (Collegeville, MN and Washington, D.C.:
   Interfaith Sexual Trauma Institute and Alban Institute, 1995).
4. *Beginning Ministry Together* by Roy M. Oswald, James M. Heath,
   and Ann W. Heath (Washington, D.C.: Alban Institute, 2003).
   This book summarizes much of Oswald's pioneering discoveries.
   See especially his concept of "The Transition Committee" (pp.
   9–10).

Bibliography

The Alban Institute has produced many helpful resources for congregations undergoing pastoral transitions. As his multiple titles listed here indicate, the work of Alban senior consultant Roy Oswald has particularly helped to define this field. The titles described below do not exhaust the resources that congregations and their leaders might find useful in navigating pastoral transitions, from Alban or otherwise, but do represent a core library of publications that address the key issues. For additional resources on pastoral transitions, visit the Congregational Resource Guide Web site (http://www.congregationalresources.org), which provides annotated listings of many more publications, organizations, and resources that will be helpful as you meet this critical moment of ministry.

Antal, James A. *Considering a New Call: Ethical and Spiritual Challenges for Clergy.* Bethesda, Md.: Alban Institute, 2000.

Written especially for the pastor who is "feeling the itch" to move to a different congregation, this book explores the sensitive issues of confidentiality and ethics as one discerns the directions of one's call and explores possibilities with other congregations.

Avery, William O. *Revitalizing Congregations: Refocusing and Healing through Pastoral Transitions.* Bethesda, Md.: Alban Institute, 2002.

As noted in this book, trained interim pastors can make all the difference in preparing the path for a ministry transition. This book tells stories of six congregations that successfully navigated this in-between time with the help of a skilled interim pastor.

Clayton, Paul C. *Letters to Lee: Mentoring the New Minister.* Bethesda, Md.: Alban Institute, 1999.

Written as a series of letters to a pastor serving his (or her) first congregation, new pastors, mentors, and congregational boards will all find this work helpful in understanding the challenges and learning curves that new pastors face.

Ketcham, Bunty. *So You're On the Search Committee.* Revised edition. Herndon, Va.: Alban Institute, 2005.

A good companion piece to the book you're holding. Ketcham, who has worked with dozens of churches in transition, not only provides practical tips to search committee members but shows unusual sensitivity to the emotional processes that accompany such changes.

Ludwig, Glenn E. *In It for the Long Haul: Building Effective Long-Term Pastorates.* Bethesda, Md.: Alban Institute, 2002.

A useful guide to both pastors and congregations on understanding the political and personal dynamics that must be navigated to enter a new church successfully and have an effective sustained ministry.

Macy, Ralph. *The Interim Pastor.* Bethesda, Md.: Alban Institute, 1986.

A good brief introduction to interim ministry and understanding its function and value to a congregation seeking a new pastor. Available online only at www.alban.org.

Nicholson, Roger S., ed. *Temporary Shepherds: A Congregational Handbook for Interim Ministry.* Bethesda, Md.: Alban Institute, 1998.

This is the standard text on interim ministry, written by a dozen experienced interim pastors. Both lay leaders and interim ministers will find this book indispensable.

Oswald, Roy M. *Crossing the Boundary between Seminary and Parish.* Bethesda, Md.: Alban Institute, 1993.

Based on an early Alban Institute research project, this document still provides essential information on understanding the challenges of moving out of the seminary environment and into congregational leadership. Available online only at www.alban.org.

————. *Ending Well, Starting Strong: Your Personal Pastorate Start-Up Workshop.* Bethesda, Md.: Alban Institute, 1995.

A set of six tapes that function as a self-guided, two-day workshop for pastors contemplating or in the midst of making a change, helping them to understand their closure styles and get a hold on the key tasks of starting up.

————. *New Beginnings: The Pastorate Start-Up Workbook.* Washington, D.C.: Alban Institute, 1989.

Oswald provides helpful resources to assist pastors understand their leadership and entry styles, to build support systems, and to do the essential self-care to overcome the stress and strain of making a transition.

————. *Running through the Thistles: Terminating a Ministerial Relationship with a Parish.* Washington, D.C.: Alban Institute, 1978.

A clear, brief exploration of termination styles and how they can effect both the pastor and the congregation.

Oswald, Roy M., and Robert E. Friedrich Jr. *Discerning Your Congregation's Future: A Strategic and Spiritual Approach.* Bethesda, Md.: Alban Institute, 1996.

Although nor written specifically for congregations undergoing a pastoral transition, this book provides useful guides to discerning where your church is being called to go, which can in turn help shape the pastoral search profile.

Oswald, Roy M., James M. Heath, and Ann W. Heath. *Beginning Ministry Together: The Alban Handbook for Clergy Transitions.* Herndon, Va.: Alban Institute, 2003.

This new resource is another essential text for churches undergoing a pastoral change, as it explores every step of the process and the key tasks that pastors, lay leaders, search committees, and judicatories must tackle to ensure successful transitions.

Rendle, Gilbert R. *Leading Change in the Congregation: Spiritual and Organizational Tools for Leaders.* Bethesda, Md.: Alban Institute, 1998.

Another book not written directly at churches undergoing pastoral changes, but a wonderful guide to understanding the dynamics of change and how it can be navigated successfully.

Rendle, Gilbert R., and Alice Mann. *Holy Conversations: Strategic Planning as a Spiritual Practice for Congregations.* Bethesda, Md.: Alban Institute, 2003.

This book is a compendium of some of the best knowledge available on designing a process not just for strategic planning but for understanding God's direction for your congregation and acting upon it.

Vonhof, John. *The Alban Guide to Managing the Pastoral Search Process.* Bethesda, Md.: Alban Institute, 1999.

An eminently practical guidebook to managing every step of the pastoral search, with great ideas on handling paperwork, working with a search team, and communicating with the congregation.

White, Edward A., ed. *Saying Goodbye: A Time of Growth for Congregations and Pastors.* Bethesda, Md.: Alban Institute, 1990.

Some of the best advice available on making a "good goodbye," which shows some keen understanding of the emotions that accompany this change. This book also includes examples of a farewell worship service and a litany for the closing of a ministry.